CREATING A WEBSITE

using

WORDPRESS

The Beginner's Guide

First Edition

The Website Series

Shere L.H. McClamb

Anna Reeves, Editor

First published: January 2016

Published by The bITa Group, LLC
Publishing@TheBitaGroup.com
Benson, North Carolina 27504

ISBN: 2370000279606

Preface

Dowloaded by thousands each year, WordPress continues to be the code-free platform of choice for millions around the world seeking to build their own website. My decision to write a book on WordPress was born out of necessity. I have spent the past 10 years creating client websites with HTML and CSS. A majority of small organizations, individuals, and entrepreneurs want a professionally developed website with the freedom to make simple updates. This was just as true for my clients, and in order to help give them greater control over future updates and a more cost efficient way to administer their websites on a daily basis, I introduced them to WordPress. However, I couldn't just throw my clients into the pool without making sure they knew how to swim, so they knew that they could come to me with questions. And they did! As I launched more and more WordPress sites, I found myself developing many instructional tutorials to support the site, and those tutorials were the first step in the journey that is this book.

I also teach WordPress, HTML, and CSS, and I've found that it was a better solution to just develop my course materials than try to find a text that I felt was worth recommending to my clients and students. I am asked all the time for my opinion of a good WordPress book to get a newbie started. After designing a new WordPress class set to start in 2016, I began reviewing existing WordPress books and found that a step-by-step manual from the beginning to launch just did not exist. Then it hit me. To solve both of these dilemmas I simply needed to write a book that was short on opinions and backstory and long on hands-on exercises that walked readers through the WordPress installation and starter process. *Creating a Website using WordPress – The Beginners Guide* became the text I had been searching for, and I knew it would be just what I needed to teach students and clients how to navigate the process of installing and getting started with WordPress.

Writing this book is a selfish endeavor in that I know it will make my life as a teacher and service provider easier. But it is also my sincere hope that it will pay dividends for anyone who has stumbled unsuccessfully through a WordPress installation or is downloading WordPress for the first time WordPress can be an awesome platform if you don't get caught with a problem that you have no idea how to fix. My past experience gained through countless formal and informal consultations over the years with frustrated clients and students tells me that, even with this book, not everyone will become instant WordPress installation wizzes. That is ok. The important thing to remember is that as long as you learn from an experience, it cannot be wholly negative. In this book, you will find an awesome reference document, and it will be able to walk you through a large number of potential trouble areas. Each process dealt with in the book is explained extensively and utilizes screen shots the entire way. I know this process works, and it can work for you!

Writing this book reiterated my sideline cheerleading for several open source applications (FileZilla, Notepad++, Linux, Apache, and MySQL) and specifically for the WordPress community. The open source approach provides a do-it-yourself alternative to website building that works. As a professional web designer, I feel more empowered sharing my process with others. The printing of this book is like my going to the top of the highest building and shouting out to the world one of my best web development secrets!

Who is this book for?

- **Individuals** with limited or no coding experience who want to build a WordPress website.
- **Instructors** who are tasked with teaching WordPress to beginners.

Conventions

The following conventions are used to walk you through building a web site using WordPress:

- Step-by-step methodology.
- Learning by building a site.
- Using open-source resources.
- Tips around known pitfalls that may hinder progress.

4

Contents

What this book covers

CHAPTER ONE: INTRODUCTION You will learn about WordPress as part of the family of open-source applications.

CHAPTER TWO: DNS, DOMAIN NAMES, AND HOSTS You will learn about domain names and hosts and how to secure them.

CHAPTER THREE: NAVIGATING THE WORDPRESS COMMUNITY AND RESOURCES You will learn about the community that maintains and supports the WordPress application.

CHAPTER FOUR: INSTALLING WORDPRESS ON A SERVER You will learn how to install WordPress, including using open source FTP clients, source code editor, and the famous 5-minute install.

CHAPTER FIVE: INSIDE WORDPRESS You will learn to navigate the WordPress dashboard that contains the functions for building your website.

CHAPTER SIX: CREATING CONTENT You will learn how to create content for your website using posts and pages.

CHAPTER SEVEN: WORKING WITH MEDIA You will learn how to use the Media Library and how to add media to your posts and pages.

CHAPTER EIGHT: SITE ORGANIZATION You will learn how to use menus to organize your site information and manage site users.

CHAPTER NINE: EXTENDING WORDPRESS BEHAVIORS You will learn how to add the functionality that will make your site unique and useful to your visitors using plugins, widgets, and themes.

CHAPTER TEN: SITE MAINTENANCE You will learn how to protect your site's information by backing up the database and updating content, files, plugins, and themes.

About the Author

Shere L.H. McClamb has more than 15 years working in the Information Technology field in the roles of Webmaster, Instructor, Instructional Technologies Developer, and Business Systems Analyst. She has taught at community and 4-year colleges as well as working for various governmental agencies within the State of North Carolina.

Shere holds a PhD in Information Technology from Capella University, develops websites and print media for her wonderful clients, teaches Web technologies to adults, and currently works full-time as a Business Systems Analyst for the North Carolina State Bureau of Investigations in Raleigh, North Carolina.

Thanks

I would like to thank my husband, Derrick, for his unwavering support for my many years of education and special projects. I would also like to thank my wonderful children (Todd, Danielle, Christopher, and Daniel) for cheering their Mom on as she stared at computer screens year after year. I would also like to thank my family, friends, and coworkers for supporting me through *another* project. –Shere

CHAPTER ONE: INTRODUCTION

If your goal is to build a WordPress site, this is a great place to start. WordPress is a free, open source content management system that allows those with no development experience to build fully functioning websites.

In this chapter, you will:

- Learn about General Public Licensed (GPL) software
- Learn the WordPress Installation requirements
- Learn about WordPress on the Web

Welcome to *Creating a Website using WordPress – The Beginner's Guide* part of *The Website Series* of books, where the goal is to equip those with limited web development experience with the skills and confidence to build a great website using the WordPress platform. Since 2003, WordPress has provided those with little web coding skills the ability to bring their websites to life. During this time, millions of users have downloaded and installed the software script WordPress to create websites for their blogs, businesses, personal entertainment, and everything in-between. WordPress powers approximately 24% of all websites on the internet today, and this number is growing every day.

Building a Website using WordPress – The Beginners Guide allows those with no web development experience to:

- Rely upon a solid foundation when building a WordPress site from the ground up.
- Create websites using WordPress that range in size from a couple of pages to complex enterprise websites that consist of hundreds of pages.
- Use the step-by-step instructions and screenshots references to help them achieve their goals of developing their first site.

Newcomers to WordPress should benefit greatly from the explanations and screenshots provided through each step in the process. Those who have attempted WordPress and have experienced obstacles they couldn't overcome can feel confident to try again knowing that they now have the support they need to launch their WordPress site.

WordPress is a Content Management System (CMS) that was initially developed as a blogging platform. It was used as a publishing vehicle by bloggers and online reporters who published information for public consumption through a weblog. In short, it allows the website creators to manage information creating, editing, and publishing content [posts and pages] in a collaborative manner [user profiles] from a central interface [the dashboard].

What makes WordPress so attractive is that it is free. It is also is easy to use once you know what you're doing, but the underlining draw is that the software itself is of no cost to the user.

The next question is understandably, how is this possible? The answer is that WordPress is an open source software licensed under a general public license (GPL). So let me answer two questions:

What is open source?

OpenSource.org defines open source software as applications that can be freely used, changed, shared by users, and distributed under a license that conforms to the open source definition (https://opensource.org/).

What is GPL?

The free software foundation (gnu.org) argues that users should not be restricted by their software, and it defines 4 specific freedoms associated with open source software use: (1) to use software for any purpose (2) to change the software to suit your needs (3) to share the software as you see fit; and finally (4) to freely share any changes you make to the software (http://www.gnu.org/licenses/gpl-3.0.en.html).

So, if it's free and anybody can do whatever they want, who is steering this ship? The code, documentation, themes, and plugins, essentially everything, is created and updated by the WordPress community. The WordPress community is made up of millions of users, developers, designers, and all-around computer geeks from all over the world! More on the benefits of this community including help, support, and community resources in chapter 2.

INSTALLATION REQUIREMENTS FOR WORDPRESS

WordPress is comprised of what is called the LAMP stack. LAMP is the acronym stands for Linux, Apache, MySQL, and PHP technologies that allow for your pages to come to life for viewers.

LAMP

All computers run on an operating system. Many of you are familiar with the more popular for-pay operating systems, Windows and Apple.

The Linux Operating System is a popular, open source version of UNIX operating System. https://www.linux.com/

L**A**MP

Your website will reside on a remote server so that the world can access your masterpiece. The software that processes the requests for your URL (web address) is the server software.

Apache Web-Server is the world's most used web server software. Originally based on the NCSA HTTPd server, development of Apache began in early 1995 after work on the NCSA code stalled. http://apache.org

LA**M**P

WordPress is a database driven site, meaning, the information for your webpages actually reside in the columns and rows of a table. Below is a sample of the database of the posts created for the website we will create during the course of this text. Web pages are assembled from the

data in the table when they are requested by the web server.

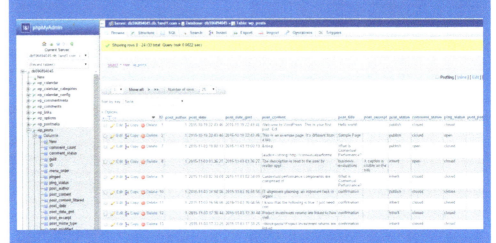

MySQL is a database for storing application information. SQL Community Edition is licensed under the GPL License and is free to download and use. https://www.mysql.com/. At this time WordPress requires **MySQL version 5.0.15 or greater** .

LAM**P**

PHP is the language in which WordPress web pages are written. It is this scripting language that gives the directions of how to assemble the pages for viewing.

PHP stands for PHP Hypertext Preprocessor. This is a server-side scripting language which is especially designed to be use in the development of websites. PHP it is now being used in more than 20,000,000 websites. http://php.net/. At this time WordPress requires **PHP version 5.2.4 or Greater.**

18

How are WordPress Sites Created?

The wordpress.org website has the link (Download WordPress) that is required to install the WordPress platform. Once you are sure the installation requirements are in place, the first step is to download the software from the wordpress.org website. The zipped file that is downloaded from the site contains all of the files you need to get started. WordPress.org also offers a community of users and developers that share instructions and tips on how to get WordPress installed, up, and running under the **Support** link on the main menu.

Installation is well-known for its straightforward process and there is even an installation help file that is downloaded with the installation files. I agree that the WordPress community has done a really great job of supporting new users by giving them the tools they need to be successful.

WHO'S USING WORDPRESS THAT I KNOW?

There are several ways to find out whether the website you are on is built with WordPress software. These include checking the source code, the site license, the URL, and usage websites. The following sections explain each different approach. Try using each different method to see who you know that uses WordPress.

The Source Code

The source code is the coding that built the website. The source code of any page on the Internet can be viewed by right-clicking anywhere on the page and choosing Source Code. The keywords **wp-content** is an indication that important files are being loaded from the **/wp-content/** folder.

The quickest way to find these keywords is to use **ctrl + f (find)**. This will bring up the find function.

Type **wp-content** into the text box.

The results show that **wp-content** is found 68 times in this document. This is definitely a site built on the WordPress platform.

Licensing

If you can view the site files of a website, there will be a license file. Try checking the license information by typing in the website's URL then **/license.txt** and see how it goes. Here's mine.

```
WordPress - Web publishing software

Copyright 2015 by the contributors

This program is free software; you can redistribute it and/or modify
it under the terms of the GNU General Public License as published by
the Free Software Foundation; either version 2 of the License, or
(at your option) any later version.
```

The URL

Check the URL of a website to see if it leads you to a WordPress login page. All websites have a domain name, to get to the dashboard to administer the website users have to log in.

 The URL for logging in to a WordPress website is the **DOMAIN NAME/wp-admin**. This is what you will see if it is a WordPress site:

Usage Websites

There are **usage** websites that are designed to identify the platforms, servers, and technologies used to build and administer a website. Builtwith.com is a popular usage website. Navigate to **http://builtwith.com**, type in the URL of the site you want more information about, and get all up in their technical business.

Try each of these approaches on my website:

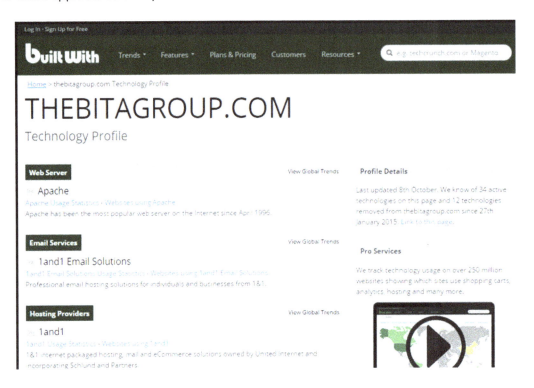

There's so much to learn, let's have some more fun.

NOTES

NOTES

CHAPTER TWO: DNS, DOMAIN NAMES, AND HOSTS

In this chapter you will learn website basics. This chapter introduces you to the more technical side of website elements you have used for years and explains the importance of carefully choosing a domain name and hosting company for your new site.

In this chapter, you will:

- Learn about the Domain Name System (DNS)
- Learn how and where to secure a domain name
- Learn how to secure the right web host

The Domain Name System (DNS) is a system that is responsible for hierarchically associating and distributing any and all resources connected to the Internet. DNS tools allow users to analyze, authenticate, and locate a domain name and email servers.

WHOis.net is a website where you can get information on website. Go to http://WhoIs.net, and enter a website URL. When a website URL is entered, the following information is returned:

Domain Name: The Top-Level Domain Name URL.

> A top-level domain is the URL or commonly the .com name for a website.

- **Registrar:** The company that registered this domain name.

> It is the responsibility of the company that sells a domain name to maintain proper registration and protect it against someone else having access to it.

- **Sponsoring Registrar IANA ID:**

> IANA is responsible for the operation and maintenance of a number of key aspects of the DNS, including the root zone, and the .int and .arpa domains.

- **Whois Server:** whois.net

> Whois.net is a reputable service to view domain information. It is wise to visit the Whois to view the registration information for a domain.

- **Name Server:** The name of the sever the domain name is serviced through.

> The host of a website will have unique internal names for the servers on their network. You will have access to your server's names as they will be required to perform certain tasks.

- **Status:** The status of the domain name according to icann.org/.

ICANN is a nonprofit organization who is responsible for the creation and management of the domain names that are accessible on the Internet.

- **Updated Date:** The dates any updates to the domain name including reissues and transfers.

  Domain names are in constant movement. They are purchased, retired, traded, and sold between individuals and companies. All of these transactions are tracked and updated with ICANN.

- **Creation Date:** The date the domain name was originally registered.

  The initial and original creation date of a top-level domain name. A domain name will only have one creation date.

- **Expiration Date:** The date the domain name is scheduled to expire, which puts the domain name back on the market where it can be sold to someone else.

  This is the date when a domain name will no longer have an owner, will not accessible on the Internet, and can be purchased.

SELECTING A DOMAIN NAME

Selecting a great domain name is an important step towards a successful website. There are many credible websites that offer domain name registrations. It is often less stressful on those who are new to dealing with domains to purchase the domain name from the same vendor who will host your site. Hosting companies usually offer domain name and hosting together in a package. If you are new to purchasing a domain name, it is recommended to take time and due diligence in researching pricing and reputation of a hosting company prior to signing up. Many times a discount or special pricing is given when a domain name is purchase bundled with web hosting space.

Top-Level Domains

Let's talk about (Top-Level) domain name extensions. Knowing the extension that best fits your website tells your users you are 'web-informed'. For example, dotcoms URLs ending in **.com** are so over and often incorrectly used.

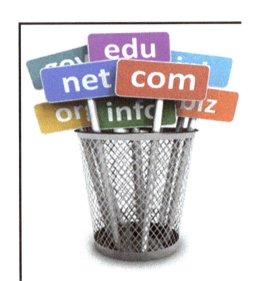

We will cover the more popular ones:

.com represents the word "commercial"

.net represents the word "network"

.org represents the word "organization"

.biz is used for "small businesses"

.info is for credible resource websites and signifies a "resource"

.mobi is short for "mobile"

.tv is for rich content/multi-media websites, commonly used within the entertainment or media industry.

.travel is used for travel and tourism industry related sites

Your domain name should adequately represent your site content. Over the years there have been many naming schemes have come and gone, but URLs that represent their entities well have stood the test of time. What if the best domain name for you is already registered? With the popularity of the internet, your second or third best choice is probably the one that is going to be available.

Don't get discouraged – domain names can be up to 67 characters (including numbers and letters) so get creative!

Securing a domain name is relatively easy and straightforward. There are several web hosts that register domain names.

Again, try to find and use the hosting company that best fit your needs by getting the most for your money. We discuss web hosts and what they provide in the next section.

WEB HOSTS

Choosing the right host for your website is important for the success of your website. A Web host is the company that houses and displays your website on demand for your visitors. Take the time to choose a hosting solution to best fit your requirements. The types of WordPress hosting options commonly available are free, shared, virtual private server (VPS), dedicated, and managed WordPress hosting.

Web hosts will often offer solutions through packages charged monthly. These packages should include the features you will need to create a WordPress website.

- Web Space
- FTP (File Transfer Protocol) Access
- MySQL Database(s)
- Traffic Volume
- Email Addresses

It is important that the hosting solution you choose has unlimited access to the elements required to install and maintain your WordPress website. It is also important for hosts to guarantee the data center that houses your site is secure and will run with as little interruption as possible. Limited downtime should be their #1 priority. The exact package you will require is based on the need of your website, so advance planning of your site will allow you make sound decisions in this area.

When Choosing a Hosting Service:

*Domain Name (required)
Most domain names are purchased from a web host. When choosing a web host, investigate the benefits of securing the domain name as part of securing the web hosting package. Many times a

generic domain name is included with the hosting package with an option to upgrade it to one of your choosing a special price.

*Web Space *(required)*

This is the space your website will take up on the hosts server. Host often divide a server into compartments of space and sell it to individuals on a monthly basis. Think of this as renting a home for your website. If you plan to have a lot of content (images, movies, music) you should plan to purchase more space than let's say a blogger who will mostly write articles containing mostly text. I understand, being new to this you probably have no idea how big your site will be or how much space you will need. Well, you can always buy more space – so no worries there.

NOTE: Do not purchase a WordPress Hosting package.

Let's start by examining the following hosting offering examples:

FTP User Profiles *(required)*

Mostly all mid-tier hosting packages come with the ability to create FTP users. WordPress files will be moved from your local computer to your web server via FTP (file transfer protocol).

*MySQL Database *(required)*

The application that stores the information of your website. This option is often omitted from the list of hosting functionality for WordPress hosting. If you do not specifically see where you can set up your own databases this is NOT the hosting package for you.

Traffic Volume

There are many hosting packages to choose from. Make sure that your package can handle the amount of traffic you anticipate for your website. As you can see in the hosting examples provided the more popular hosts offer more space than you will ever use. Still take the time to ensure you have the right amount of space for your website needs.

Email Addresses

The email addresses supplied through your host will provide @YourDomainName for a professional and polished look.

Web Hosts

Below are just a few of the many web hosts available to choose from.

1&1
http://www.1and1.com/
{Recommended by Me}

Bluehost
http://www.bluehost.com/
{Recommended by the WordPress}

Dreamhost
https://www.dreamhost.com/

HostGator
http://www.hostgator.com/

Inmotion Hosting
https://www.inmotionhosting.com/

Siteground
https://www.siteground.com/

NOTES

NOTES

CHAPTER THREE: NAVIGATING THE WORDPRESS COMMUNITY AND RESOURCES

> *This chapter introduces you to the WordPress website and community and discusses the help and support of the Codex.*

In this chapter, you will:

- Learn the difference between WordPress.org and WordPress.com
- Learn about the power of the Codex
- Learn about the importance of the WordPress community

WordPress.org is the open source website that offers a free download of the WordPress software, themes, plugins, and support. Whereas, Wordpress.com is a commercial web hosting site operated by Matt Mullenweg, a co-founder of the open source WordPress software that allows users to create websites using the WordPress software. Hosting a site on wordpress.com is free, but extending the functionality of the site results in a fee.

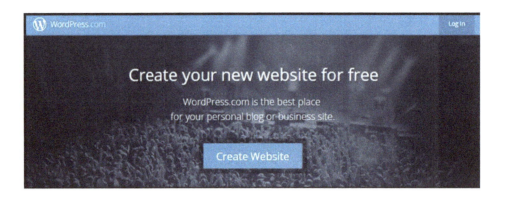

THE CODEX

The WordPress Codex is the user manual and support documentation in wiki form for WordPress software. The Codex has information on how to use and troubleshoot the WordPress application, themes, and plugins. The WordPress Codex URL is: https://codex.wordpress.org/.

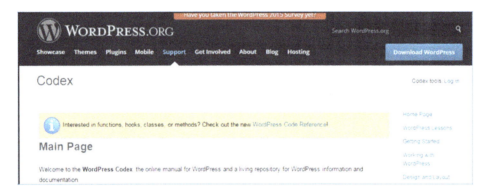

HELP & SUPPORT

Help and support can also be found in the Codex. The help page is broken into three sections: Help for Everyone, Help for Readers, and Help for Editors. Resources for everyone from beginners to developers are available in the Codex.

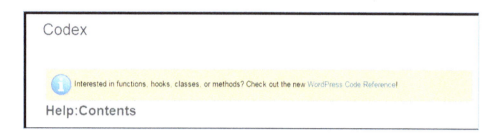

THE WORDPRESS COMMUNITY

There is also access to the community portal in the Codex. This includes information on:

- Previous, current, and upcoming releases;
- Changes; installations; and
- Upgrades.

The WordPress community is open, and anyone is free to contribute to its ongoing success.

Codex:Contributing

Languages: 中文(简体) • Deutsch • **English** • Español • Français • Italiano • 日本語 • 한국어 • Português do Brasil • ไทย • Türkçe • (Add your language)

Welcome

The Codex is a wiki, meaning anyone can edit it. It grows and thrives off of individual contributions from people like you. Thank you for choosing to contribute to the Codex This page should show you several ways in which you can contribute to the WordPress documentation project at the Codex

Contents

NOTES

CHAPTER FOUR: INSTALLING WORDPRESS ON A SERVER

This chapter covers the installation of the WordPress software to your remote server or local machine. It also covers additional applications such as FTP clients and source code editors needed during the installation process.

In this chapter, you will:

- Use the Notepad++ code editing application to prepare your local WordPress files
- Use the Filezilla FTP client to upload your local WordPress files to your remote server
- Prepare your mySQL Database
- Create a remote directory
- Run the famous 5-minute install

In this chapter we will set the foundation required to install WordPress on a remote (hosted web server). Hosting companies understand the popularity of WordPress, and as a result, they generally offer one-click installs to their customers.

I have found that for many sites this is not ideal. First, it can make it more difficult for the business owner to access certain files, and it can also lower upload capacities on image files. Because this may cause problems once the site is up, it is important understand how a one-click install may impact your website down the line.

One-Click Installation Methods

Each hosting company approaches one-click WordPress installation differently, and as a result, specific one-click instructions vary from hosting company to hosting company. Visit WordPress Web Hosting at https://wordpress.org/hosting/ to read more on WordPress community recommendations.

Below are popular examples. If you decide to use this installation method, your host will provide all of the information you require to get through it.

Some one-click installation methods are easier than others. Some are not one-click at all. They end up being... Click and do the rest yourself. The procedures for one-click installation of WordPress are NOT covered in this text.

1and1.com offers Quick Website creation through the App Center in the Control Panel.

Bluehost offers One-click Install through the Mojo Marketplace.

Dreamhost offers a One-Click Install through Goodies in the Panel.

These examples should give you some idea about the one-click installs. If your site will be very simple and require minimal updating, smaller image sizes, or limited customized plugins and widgets, the one-click install is an alternative to explore. However, one of the goals of this book is to help people understand the WordPress installation process in its entirety.

So let's get started on a custom install!

INSTALLATION PREPRARATION

There are several items that need to be taken care of prior to installation:

Installation of a source code editor – This example will use Notepad++

Installation of a FTP Client – This example will use Filezilla

Preparation of the WordPress Website Directory - The WordPress application files need to be moved to your local website folder. You will create the directory through your web host.

Create a FTP User - You need to create a user that will administer the transfer of files from the local and remote servers. You will create the directory through your web host.

Creation of a Database and a User - You need to create your MySql database and username for the installation. You will create the database through your web host.

MySQL Database – Configuration File - WordPress stores your database information in the wp-config.php file. Without this information, your WordPress website will not work, and you will get the 'error establishing database connection' error.

NOTEPAD++ SOURCE CODE EDITOR

The WordPress configuration file and other text file will need to be opened and edited in a text editor. Notepad++ is a free and open sourced text editor.

STEP 1.   Navigate to https://notepad-plus-plus.org/.

STEP 2.   Click the **download** link or button.

Result: The download screen appears.

STEP 3.   Click the oval download button.

Result: The file will download to your computer.

STEP 4. Choose the language from the dropdown menu.

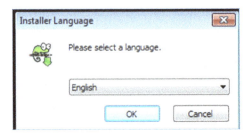

STEP 5. Click the **Next** button to work through the installer instructions.

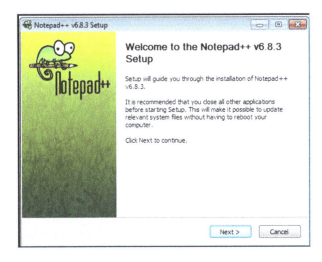

STEP 6.   Accept the Terms of Agreement by clicking on the **I Agree** button.

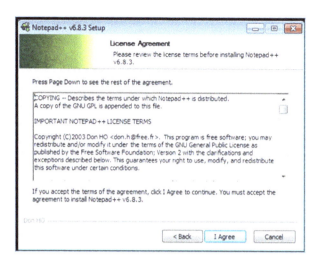

STEP 7.   You will probably NOT need to alter the destination folder.

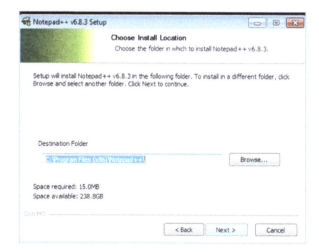

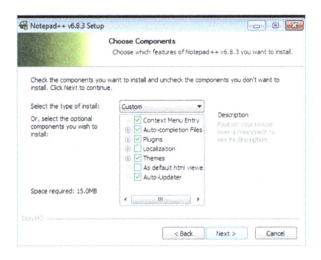

STEP 8.   It is good to start with the components that are checked by default.

STEP 9.   ONLY check the option to place a shortcut on your desktop.

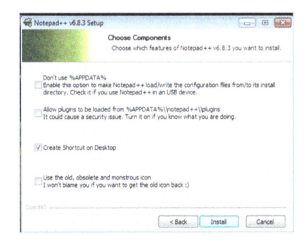

STEP 10.   Click the **Install** button.

STEP 11.   Click the **Finish** button.

> **Result:** Notepad++ is now installed
> on your computer.

STEP 12.   Open Notepad++.

STEP 13. Create and save a
WebSiteInformation.txt to record
important information to be used
later in the installation process.

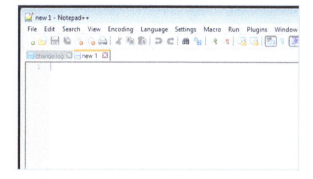

UPLOADING WORDPRESS FILES TO YOUR WEB SERVER

File Transfer Protocol (FTP)

This step in the process involves moving the files from your local computer to your web server. The process used to move files on the Internet is called the File Transfer Protocol (FTP). What distinguishes FTP from most other protocols is the use of secondary connections for file transfers.

There are two file locations that we will concern ourselves with:

Local Files

Local files are the files that live in the directories on your computer or thumb drive.

Remote Files

Remote files are the files that live on the web server.

When you connect to an FTP server, you are actually making two connections.

1. A control connection is established, over which FTP commands and their replies are transferred.

2. To transfer a file or a directory listing, the client sends a particular command over the control connection to establish the data connection.

The data connection will be established passive mode. Using passive mode, the client sends the PASV command to the server, and the server responds with an address. The client then issues a command to transfer a file or to get a directory listing and establishes a secondary connection to the address returned by the server.

FTP Clients

 WinSCP {Windows} A free, open source FTP, SFTP, SCP and FTPS client known as the most powerful and easy to use FTP client for Windows users.

 FireFTP {Windows | Mac | Linux} A free, secure, cross-platform FTP/SFTP client for the Mozilla Firefox browser. FireFTP is a Mozilla Firefox add-on, so the user experience is seamless because FireFTP blends into the web browser. You need the Mozilla Firefox browser to use it.

 FileZilla {Windows} A popular free FTP clients for Windows that is available on all other platforms as well. It has been reported that adware and/or spyware was downloaded with the FileZilla download. You can uncheck the boxes during the installation to remove any extra functionality you may not need.

 Transmit {Mac} The most popular FTP client for Mac, particularly among web developers. Transmit at a cost per license.

 CyberDuck {Windows | Mac} Free and open source FTP, SFTP, WebDAV, Rackspace Cloud Files, Google Docs, Windows Azure & Amazon S3 software for use with Mac and Windows.

 **gFTP** {Linux}
An open source FTP client for Linux-based operating systems.

INSTALLING THE Filezilla FTP CLIENT

STEP 1. Navigate to the Filezilla main page - https://filezilla-project.org/

STEP 2. Click the **Download FileZilla Client** button.

STEP 3. Click the **Download Now** button.

Result: The download should start automatically. If it does not, click the **Start Download** button.

STEP 4.   Once your download is complete, you will receive a thank you message. **Close this page.**

STEP 5.   Click on the zipped '**executable**' file. Options to run the file will appear.

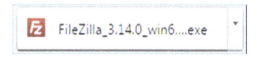

STEP 6.   Click the **Run** button.

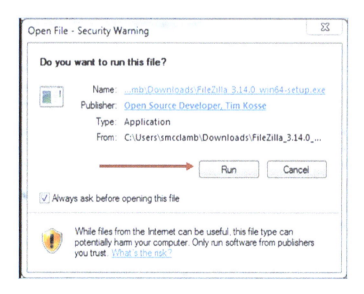

STEP 7.   Click the **Yes** button. You want the Filezilla FTP Client to make the necessary changes to your computer.

STEP 8.   Click the **I Agree** button to accept the terms of agreement with Filezilla.

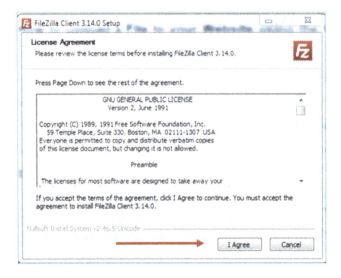

STEP 9.   Select the **Anyone who uses this computer (all users)** option if it is not already selected. Click the **Next** button.

STEP 10.   Place a checkmark in **ALL** of the components to install and click the **Next** button.

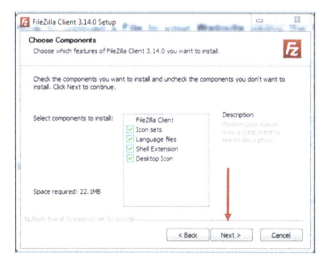

STEP 11.   In most cases, you do not need to change the destination folder. Click the **Next** button.

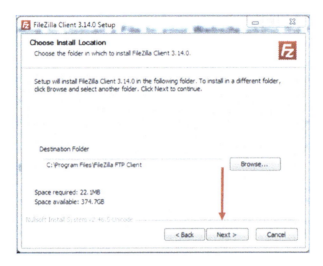

STEP 12.   Use the default **Filezilla FTP Client** folder listed, just click the **Install** button.

STEP 13.   Click the **Finish** button to complete the install.

Result: The Filezilla FTP Client will open with a message: **Welcome to FileZilla**.

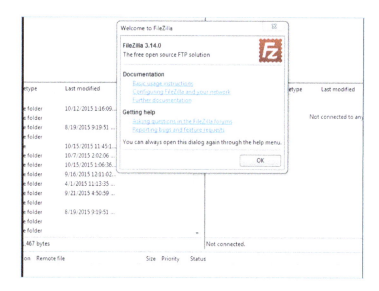

You Have Successfully Downloaded and Opened the FileZilla FTP Client!

DOWNLOADING WORDPRESS FILES

The Website Local Folder

Next, WordPress files will have to be downloaded to your computer from WordPress.org, unzipped, configured, and uploaded to your web server.

STEP 1.   Go to http://wordpress.org/.

STEP 2.   Click the **Download WordPress x.x.x** button in the top right hand of the screen.

STEP 3.   Click **Download WordPress x.x** (the latest version).

Result: The WordPress file will be downloaded to your computer.

STEP 4.   Choose the folder on your computer where the WP zipped file will be saved. Create a new folder if you need to.

STEP 5.   Complete the download.

Result: These files will be downloaded into a zipped file.

Unzip the WordPress File

STEP 1.   Navigate to the zipped file.

STEP 2.   Right-click to bring up the short-cut menu and choose **Extract All**.

STEP 3.   Select the directory where you wish to save the WordPress files by clicking on the **Browse** button.

STEP 4.   Navigate to where you wish to save your WordPress files.

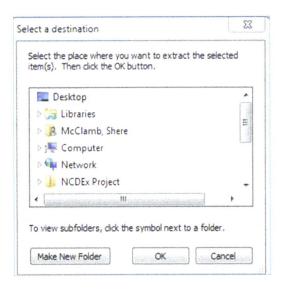

STEP 5.   Click the **Extract** button.

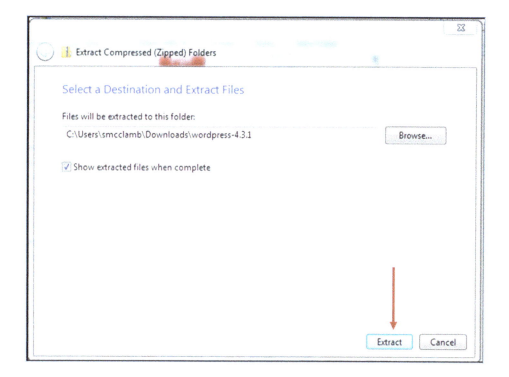

Result: The files are extracted from the zipped file and into a folder labeled **WordPress**.

THE WORDPRESS FOLDERS AND FILES

The contents of this folder perform very different tasks, and they all are very important, especially during the maintenance of the website. Let's look at the contents of the WordPress software package:

Name	Type	Size
wp-admin	File folder	
wp-content	File folder	
wp-includes	File folder	
index.php	PHP File	1 KB
license.txt	Text Document	20 KB
readme.html	Chrome HTML Do...	8 KB
wp-activate.php	PHP File	5 KB
wp-blog-header.php	PHP File	1 KB
wp-comments-post.php	PHP File	5 KB
wp-config-sample.php	PHP File	3 KB
wp-cron.php	PHP File	4 KB
wp-links-opml.php	PHP File	3 KB
wp-load.php	PHP File	4 KB
wp-login.php	PHP File	34 KB
wp-mail.php	PHP File	9 KB
wp-settings.php	PHP File	11 KB
wp-signup.php	PHP File	25 KB
wp-trackback.php	PHP File	4 KB
xmlrpc.php	PHP File	3 KB

Folders (Directory)

wp-admin: The files in this folder control the administration of the WordPress website and are known commonly as Admin.

wp-content: This folder contains the themes (the files that control the way your site looks) and the plugins (the files that extend functionality) used to create your site.

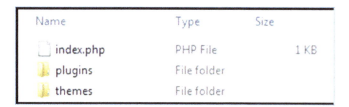

wp-includes: This folder contains the workhorse files, php files that tell your site what to do, how to do it, and when it should be done.

certificates	category-template.php	class-wp-customize-manager.php
css	class.wp-dependencies.php	class-wp-customize-nav-menus.php
fonts	class.wp-scripts.php	class-wp-customize-panel.php
ID3	class.wp-styles.php	class-wp-customize-section.php
images	class-feed.php	class-wp-customize-setting.php
js	class-http.php	class-wp-customize-widgets.php
pomo	class-IXR.php	class-wp-editor.php
SimplePie	class-json.php	class-wp-embed.php
Text	class-oembed.php	class-wp-error.php
theme-compat	class-phpass.php	class-wp-http-ixr-client.php
admin-bar.php	class-phpmailer.php	class-wp-image-editor.php
atomlib.php	class-pop3.php	class-wp-image-editor-gd.php
author-template.php	class-simplepie.php	class-wp-image-editor-imagick.php
bookmark.php	class-smtp.php	class-wp-theme.php
bookmark-template.php	class-snoopy.php	class-wp-walker.php
cache.php	class-wp.php	class-wp-xmlrpc-server.php
canonical.php	class-wp-admin-bar.php	comment.php
capabilities.php	class-wp-ajax-response.php	comment-template.php
category.php	class-wp-customize-control.php	compat.php

Root-Level Files Explained

index.php

The index is your websites landing page. It loads the wp-blog-header.php, which tells WordPress to load the installed theme.

*license.txt:

Earlier, the book discussed navigating to the license files when determining whether a website was WordPress driven? Well here that same text is from inside the WordPress application.

```
wordPress - web publishing software

Copyright 2015 by the contributors

This program is free software; you can redistribute it and/or modify
it under the terms of the GNU General Public License as published by
the Free Software Foundation; either version 2 of the License, or
(at your option) any later version.
```

readme.html

This HTML document provides important information relevant to installing and using WordPress.

wp-activate.php

This php scripted document confirms that the activation key sent via email after a user signs up for a new blog matches the key for that user. When it does, a confirmation is displayed: confirmation.wp-blog-header.php.

wp-blog-header.php

This php scripted document loads the WordPress environment and template.

wp-comments-post.php

This php scripted document controls comment posts to WordPress and prevents duplicates.

wp-config-sample.php

This php scripted document refers to the base configuration for WordPress. The wp-config.php creation script uses this file during the installation.

wp-cron.php

This php scripted document is the root file of the WordPress Cron Implementation for hosts, which do not offer CRON or for which the user has not set up a CRON job pointing to this file. *Basically this file is used for scheduled jobs.*

wp-links-opml.php

This php scripted document is used to export links from one blog over to another. Links are not exported by the WordPress export, so this file handles that.

wp-load.php

This php scripted document used for setting the ABSPATH constant and loading the wp-config.php file. The wp-config.php file will then load the wp-settings.php file, which will then set up the WordPress environment.

wp-login.php

This php scripted document root file brings up the WordPress User Page. It handles authentication, registering, resetting passwords, and provides a forgotten password function.

wp-mail.php

This php scripted document allows for an email message from the user's mailbox to be used as a WordPress post.

wp-settings.php

This php scripted document is used to set up and fix common procedural and class library variables.

wp-sign-up.php

This php scripted document is responsible for setting up the WordPress Environment.

wp-trackback.php

This php scripted document takes care of Trackbacks and Pingbacks Sent to posts in WordPress.

xmlrpc.php

This php scripted document handles browser-embedded clients and cookies.

CREATING A CONFIGURATION FILE FOR YOUR WEBSITE

The first major step in installing the files you downloaded to your computer to the remote (hosting) server is to create the configuration file that tells WordPress the:

- URL for your site;
- username and password to access the information stored in your database;
- names of the server where your website files will be stored; and
- security for your website.

The configuration file is written in the php scripting language, so you are not expected to understand everything that is going on in this document. Required items of the configuration file are color-coded for ease in updating.

- **Green** text contain are instructions.
- Gray text wrapped in single quotations is where you will place your information.
- Updated text will turn orange once the configuration information is entered.

Setting up and properly saving the configuration file is the number one cause of issues during the installation process. Do not alter any other text in this file.

If the configuration file is does not contain these separate pieces of information, you will not be able to successfully complete the installation process. If you make a mistake during this process, close the file and start over with the wp-config-sample file.

The information required for the configuration file can be found in the **WebSiteInformation.txt** file you have developed.

STEP 1.   Open the **wp-config-sample** file in Notepad++. You should also have the **WebSiteInformation.txt** file with your database information open.

```
// ** MySQL settings - You can get this info from your web host ** //
/** The name of the database for WordPress */
define('DB_NAME', 'database_name_here');  Step 2

/** MySQL database username */
define('DB_USER', 'username_here');  Step 3

/** MySQL database password */
define('DB_PASSWORD', 'password_here');  Step 4

/** MySQL hostname */
define('DB_HOST', 'localhost');  Step 5

/** Database Charset to use in creating database tables. */
define('DB_CHARSET', 'utf8');  Step 6

/** The Database Collate type. Don't change this if in doubt. */
define('DB_COLLATE', '');
```

STEP 2.   **Go to the section labeled Step 2 of the config file sample above:**

/** The name of the database for WordPress */

define('DB_NAME', 'database_name_here');database name

STEP 3.   **Go to the section labeled Step 3 of the config file sample above:**

/** MySQL database username */

define('DB_USER', 'username_here');

STEP 4.   **Go to the section labeled Step 4 of the config file sample above:**

/** MySQL database password */

define('DB_PASSWORD', 'password_here');

STEP 5.   **Go to the section labeled Step 5 of the config file sample above:**

/** MySQL hostname */

define('DB_HOST', 'localhost');

STEP 6. **Go to the section labeled Step 6 of the config file sample above:**

/** Database Charset to use in creating database tables. */

define('DB_CHARSET', 'utf8');

Authentication Unique Keys and Salts

Authentication unique keys and salts are security keys that help improve security of your WordPress site.

WordPress Security Keys

These security keys makes it harder to crack your password. WordPress Security Keys are a set of random variables that improve encryption of information stored in the user's cookies. There are a total of four security keys: AUTH_KEY, SECURE_AUTH_KEY, LOGGED_IN_KEY, and NONCE_KEY

STEP 1. Navigate to https://api.wordpress.org/secret-key/1.1/salt/

```
←  →  C  🏠    🔒 https://api.wordpress.org/secret-key/1.1/salt/

define('AUTH_KEY',        'vNOi33jpKd@-!*$PI1.mBEcwT{}ks)83=p7`Qj4|:LzrT^43w``s.C$O%8K=L_#|');
define('SECURE_AUTH_KEY', 'Y.(X}5c+e_OV/h@1(dc@?LP0K8Coi@?iB-qS(Ng&Um(jXN?_S,eHfPxP%99xt7YL');
define('LOGGED_IN_KEY',   'U[1GBuGlD$K(SLJ=wX:MKGh- JNHTiZa3Pst[Wqr-!{=0(Hk4{4|ZLy!8IVm+Vy!');
define('NONCE_KEY',       'Yhw3]}-9$Z!6#oD}|Jw#cHEat`=?#p7uH f|EzwsdDT#&+S6Hq4{,.;YUn6|p7p,');
define('AUTH_SALT',       '+5<UcR^3YPlKCvovR (bW:q&A4Q&# .Yo(qLRfkbtd&Ru]hW1p(p)1(IC-+]:31 ');
define('SECURE_AUTH_SALT','t%@R^Y/u&aoyde%W}.Lf?3T,l^1OYc/xvE,o<YW!3|1XznY ::@4v3q=(VjA-M-s');
define('LOGGED_IN_SALT',  'YUkS[9y$T;8cBK-DJ&U-nj-^|`9b16LuMLiN|UoWG}yR+_-RE/St =^XJw,+c @k');
define('NONCE_SALT',      'I|-EVn|jZ>+teK`r|7,:wKn{1rHk[dRLlvd!/0nQMX7t8mEAK@c0wo~}Rz>dEzC*');
```

STEP 2. Copy all of the text.

```
@since 2.0.0
*/

define('AUTH_KEY',         'put your unique phrase here');
define('SECURE_AUTH_KEY',  'put your unique phrase here');
define('LOGGED_IN_KEY',    'put your unique phrase here');
define('NONCE_KEY',        'put your unique phrase here');
define('AUTH_SALT',        'put your unique phrase here');
define('SECURE_AUTH_SALT', 'put your unique phrase here');
define('LOGGED_IN_SALT',   'put your unique phrase here');
define('NONCE_SALT',       'put your unique phrase here');
```

STEP 3. Paste the copied text, into the configuration sample file replacing original the text.

```
define('AUTH_KEY',        'vNOi33jpKd@-!*$PI1.mBEcwT{}ks)83=p7`Qj4|:LzrT^43w``s.C$O%8K=L_#|');
define('SECURE_AUTH_KEY', 'Y.(X}5c+e_OV/h@1(dc@?LP0K8Coi@?iB-qS(Ng&Um(jXN?_S,eHfPxP%99xt7YL');
define('LOGGED_IN_KEY',   'U[1GBuGlD$K(SLJ=wX:MKGh- JNHTiZa3Pst[Wqr-!{=0(Hk4{4|ZLy!8IVm+Vy!');
define('NONCE_KEY',       'Yhw3]}-9$Z!6#oD}|Jw#cHEat`=?#p7uH f|EzwsdDT#&+S6Hq4{,.;YUn6|p7p,');
define('AUTH_SALT',       '+5<UcR^3YPlKCvovR (bW:q&A4Q&# .Yo(qLRfkbtd&Ru]hW1p(p)1(IC-+]:31 ');
define('SECURE_AUTH_SALT','t%@R^Y/u&aoyde%W}.Lf?3T,l^1OYc/xvE,o<YW!3|1XznY ::@4v3q=(VjA-M-s');
define('LOGGED_IN_SALT',  'YUkS[9y$T;8cBK-DJ&U-nj-^|`9b16LuMLiN|UoWG}yR+_-RE/St =^XJw,+c @k');
define('NONCE_SALT',      'I|-EVn|jZ>+teK`r|7,:wKn{1rHk[dRLlvd!/0nQMX7t8mEAK@c0wo~}Rz>dEzC*');
```

Database Table Prefix

WordPress Database is like a brain for your entire WordPress site. Every single piece of information relevant to your website is stored in there, making it hacker's favorite target. Spammers and hackers run automated codes for SQL injections. It is recommended that you change your WordPress database table prefix to something random. By default, WordPress adds wp_ prefix to all the tables created by WordPress.

```
/**
 * WordPress Database Table prefix.
 *
 * You can have multiple installations in one database if you give each
 * a unique prefix. Only numbers, letters, and underscores please!
 */
$table_prefix  = 'wp_';

/**
```

STEP 4.   It is recommended that you change your WordPress database table prefix to something random. Change the table prefix line from wp_ to something else like this wp_a123456_ **Note:** You can only change it to numbers, letters, and underscores.

STEP 5.   Click File – Save As '**wp-config.php**' and click '**Save**' in the same folder with the sample file.

That's it – You're done with the changes to the config file!

INSTALLING WORDPRESS ON A REMOTE SERVER

Uploading WordPress Files to the Remote Server

Even though FTP client interfaces are different, these basic steps should cover any of them. For this demonstration Filezilla will be used to move local folders and files from your computer to you remote server using the information from:

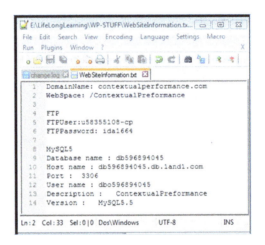

- Domain Name URL
- Directory Name
- MySQL Database Information
- FTP Account (Username and Password)

It is good practice to gather all of the information that you will need in a Notepad++ file. This will save you time and frustration when you are ready to enter the required information into the config file and the FTP client.

Domain Names and Web Space

There is information that is required for the FTP client to connect to your web server.

The hosting (DNS Settings) information is located in your host's control panel. Log in to the dashboard homepage and navigate to the domain name section.

A directory folder to hold the website files needs to be created for the domain name. The following steps are used for the 1and1.com control panel, but they should be similar in the control panel of almost any chosen host.

STEP 1.   Click the **Create Directory** button.

STEP 2.   Type in a **directory name**. Use the name of the website being created. Keep it short and sweet.

 Do not use spaces or special characters when creating the directory name.

STEP 3.   The new directory is now in the directory list. Click the **Save** button.

Result: The Web Space is now updated in the domain dashboard.

Securing an FTP Account

Manage the connections to your webspace with an FTP username and password. This should be found in a section of your host's dashboard to manage your webspace.

STEP 1.   Click the **FTP** option (Secure FTP Account).

STEP 2. Follow the instructions to create a new FTP User.

STEP 3. Fill out the information to create a new FTP user.

STEP 4. Remember, this information is case sensitive! Click the **Save** button.

Result: A FTP user account is created.

STEP 5. Record the MySQL Database information in the Website Information document in Notepad++.

MySQL Creation – Creating a Database for your Website

It is now to create what is commonly known as the brain of the WordPress website. The database is a function of your web host so you will have to log in to your web host's dashboard to create it. The procedure for creating a database will vary between webhosts, but it should be a pretty straightforward process. This text covers the creation of a new database through the 1and1.com interface.

If you run into problems locating where or how to create a database with your webhost, use their internal search feature. Mostly all of the web hosts recommended in this book has step by step instructions available.

Let's get started creating the database:

STEP 1.   Click the **MySQL Database** option.

STEP 2. Click the **New Database** button.

STEP 3. Fill out the information to create a new database.

Make sure the password for the database is SECURE using a variation of uppercase letters, lowercase letters, numbers, and symbols!

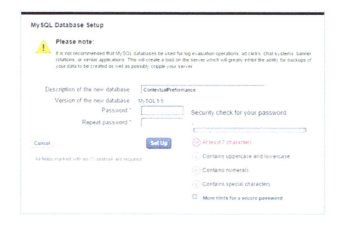

STEP 4.   Once you have completed this screen, click the **Set Up** button.

STEP 5.   Click the **Go To Overview** button.

STEP 6.   Record the MySQL Database information in the Website Information document in Notepad++.

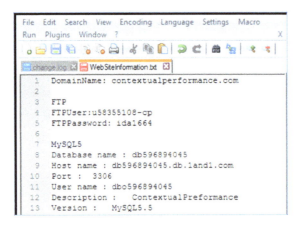

Port Numbers

A port number is associated with the transmission (movement) of a requested file (web page) from a web host. 21 is the port number associated with an unsecure FTP request. An unsecure web page request is one that does not require any additional security to access and are as is the most common on the Internet. 22 is the port number associated with a secure FTP request. As example of a secure request would be a bank, credit card company, etc.

Using the FileZilla Quick Connect Bar

STEP 1.   Fill in the information in the quick connect bar.

Host- This is you domain name or URL	**Port:** The Port for Secure FTP is 22
Username: This is your FTP Username	**Password:** This is your FTP User Password

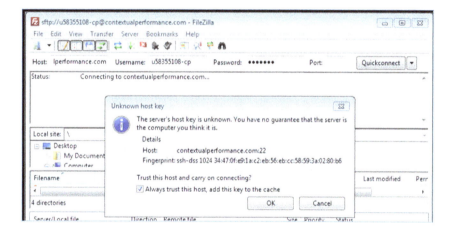

STEP 2. Make sure to check **Always trust this host, add this key to the cache**. Then click the **OK** button.

STEP 3. Click the **Quickconnect** button to connect to the server.

Result: Once established, the connection can be used for uploading or downloading site files.

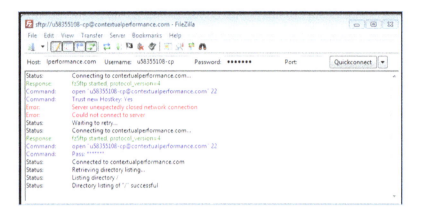

Local and Remote Files in the FTP Client

Local files are located on the left side of the interface and the remote files will be uploaded to the right side.

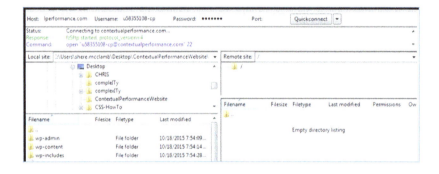

STEP 1.   Drag the your **FILES** – not your WordPress **FOLDER** (ContextualPerformance) over to the right side under **Remote site**. You will see the file movement and status updates in the top window. This transfer will take a few minutes.

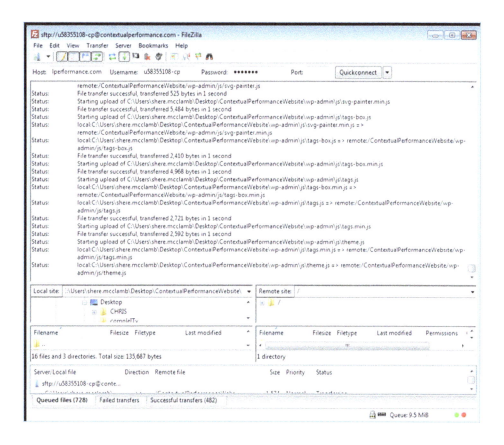

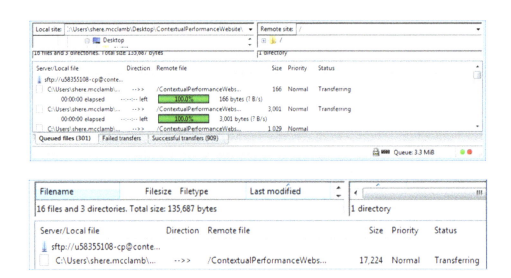

Result: The local files are now on the remote server.

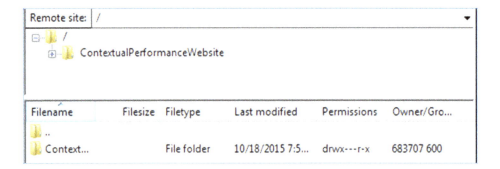

You have successfully transferred the WordPress files to the remote server!

THE FAMOUS 5-MINUTE INSTALL

Run the install script - You are now ready for the WordPress magic!

STEP 1. Go to http://yourdomain.com.   STEP 2. Fill in the WordPress setup page information.

- **Site Title**- Your WebSite Title.
- **Admin Username** – The username you will use to log into WordPress.
- **Password**- The password you will use to log into WordPress.
- **Your Email** – The email address that will be used for notifications.
- Choose whether you want your site to be indexed by search engines - **Yes**.
- Click **Install WordPress**, and you you're almost there!

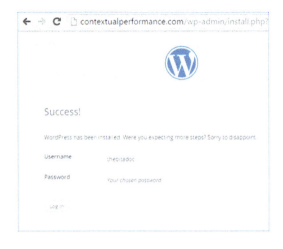

Result: You will receive an email from WordPress confirming the creation of your new site.

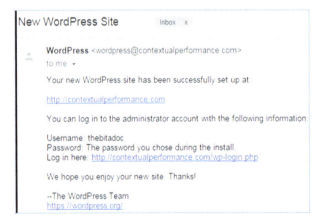

STEP 3.   Click the **Log In** ↑ and then **Log In** ↓ button and let the fun begin!

Congratulations! You've successfully installed WordPress!

NOTES

NOTES

CHAPTER FIVE: NAVIGATING WORDPRESS

You have successfully installed the WordPress software on your remote server, and now it is time to log in and familiarize yourself with the WordPress Dashboard.

In this chapter, you will:

- Learn how to log into your new site
- Learn how to navigate the WordPress dashboard
- Learn how to configure the settings for your site
- Learn how to customize your dashboard widgets using drag and drop

The customizations required for creating your site are located in the WordPress dashboard. You will need to log in to the dashboard to customize your new site.

LOGGING IN TO THE DASHBOARD

To log into your new site, type the URL, a forward slash, and then either admin, login, or wp-admin in the URL bar of your web browser.

Try It:

www.YourSite.com/admin/

or

www.YourSite.com/login/

or

www.YourSite.com/wp-admin/

All three of these URLs will redirect you to the WordPress login page. If you encounter login issues, use: **www.YourSite.com/wp-login.php.** If you will use the same personal computer to access your website, consider checking the **remember me** checkbox. This option will fill in the username and password on the login page automatically when you open the login page.

THE DASHBOARD HOMEPAGE

Congratulations again on making it this far! Manually installing WordPress is no small feat! Now, let's get familiar with the WordPress Dashboard homepage. Everyone will see this same landing page, but it is here that every website owner goes their separate ways in regards to the design and complexity of their website.

THE DASHBOARD MENU

When you Click the Screen Options tab, the resulting screen shows the various Dashboard widgets with a check-box next to each widget. Check the box for each widget you want displayed, or uncheck boxes to hide widgets.

CUSTOMIZING YOUR SITE

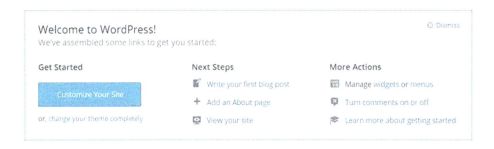

STEP 1.   Click the change your site completely link. You will be taken to the themes page.

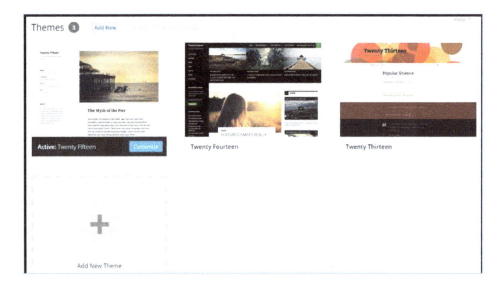

You can either customize the default theme that was installed or install one of the others.

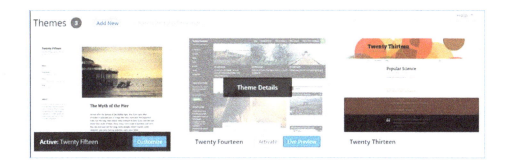

We will customize the Twenty Fifteen theme. Hover over and click each to view the theme's details.

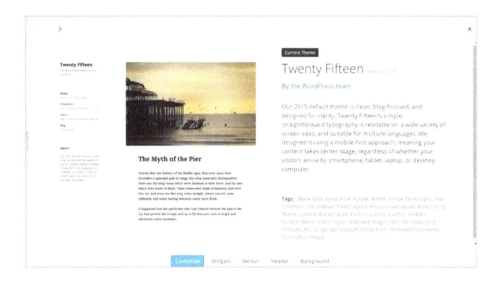

STEP 2.   Click the **Customize** button.

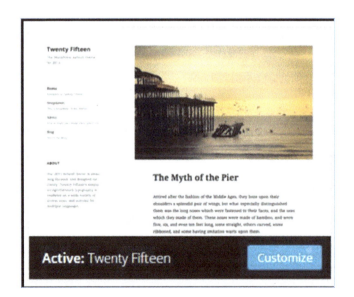

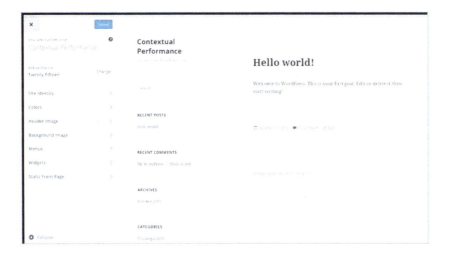

STEP 3.   Open your website in another tab so that you can view your changes with a refresh.

STEP 4.   Hover over your site name and then Click **Visit Site**.

To have your dashboard open in one page or tab and your webpage in the other – right-Click **Visit Site** and choose **open in new tab**.

Result: Your new website is opened in the web browser.

CONFIGURING WORDPRESS SETTINGS

WordPress General Settings

The general settings are pretty explanatory, and most of them were determined during the install, but there are a few items that need to be clarified.

Site Title: The WordPress site title was configured during the install, but it can be changed at any time. The site title should be short and exact as in most cases it will be visible to site visitors.

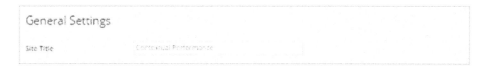

Tagline: The tagline of the site should range from a few words to one sentence. What is the site going to be known for? Think of the tag lines well-known companies and organizations use:

Like a Rock, 30 Minutes or Less, Protect and Serve. Get it?

WordPress Address (URL)

Email Address: This is a very important address. Information about the WordPress application, updates, upgrades, comment moderation, etc. will be sent to this address.

Membership: Unless you intend to pre-plan and control users by signing them up yourself, I would leave this checked. You can always delete users at a later time.

New User Default Role: When a visitor of your site decides to sign up or register, this will be the role they are automatically assigned. It is recommended that they are initially assigned to the role with the fewest rights which is the **Subscriber**.

Time Zone: Click the dropdown list to choose the time zone that you want for your web site. Think of your audience when choosing your time zone.

Date Format: The date format chosen here will show on each of the posts in your site.

Time Format: The chosen time format will show for each post in your site.

Week Starts On: Choose which day the week will start on for your website. Although the most common is Sunday, many site geared towards work-weeks start on Monday.

Site Language: WordPress does not offer support languages other than English with the install, however with the use of plugins does allow for language switching using this option.

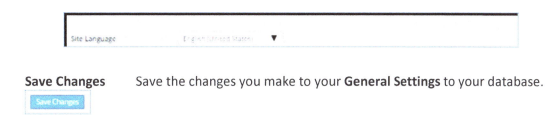

Save Changes   Save the changes you make to your **General Settings** to your database.

WordPress Writing Settings

Writing settings contains the controls for composing new posts.

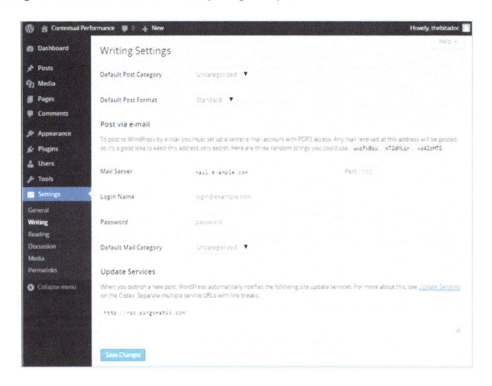

Default Post Category: Remember, WordPress was initially a blogging tool. All posts that are in the **Default Post Category** will show on the template blog page by default. You will learn how to create new categories for posts in the Posts section of the text.

Default Post Format: The default post format is relayed on the right side of each post screen. This can be changed on the post screen. When creating a post, you will see it has your choice as the default.

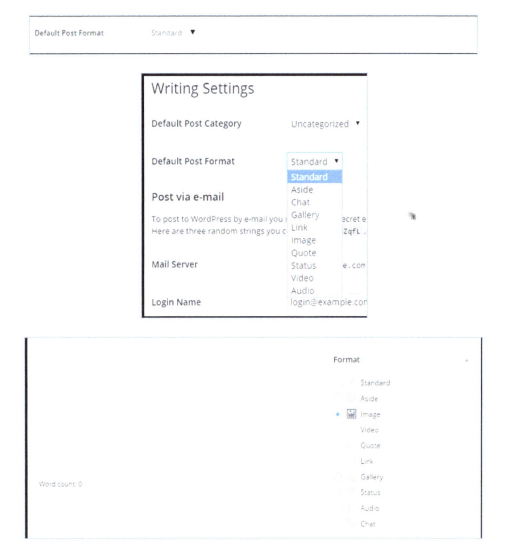

Post via e-mail: This is an option that allows you to publish content to your posts from your e-mails. In order to utilize this option, it must be enabled. To post via email, you send an e-mail to a specific address with POP3 access that you've established for the purpose. This option requires updating settings with the login name, password, and default mail category.

Update Services: Update Services allows you to notify others that you have updated your blog. You simply insert the URLs of the update services you wish to notify.

Save Changes   This allows you to save the changes you make to your **Writing Settings**.

Save Changes

WordPress Reading Settings

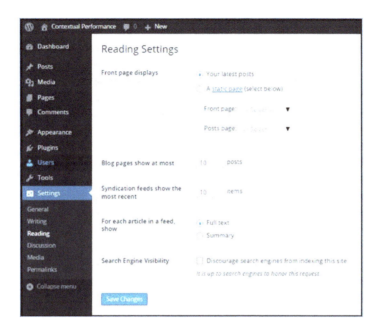

Front Page Settings: This setting allows you to control the content on your site's homepage. The question here is do you want to create a page of elements or do you want the WordPress application to put the posts that are created on the homepage? If you want WordPress to place dynamic content on the homepage, there are some follow-up questions that need to answer. How many blog posts do you want to show? Do you want the syndication feeds show the most recent? Do you want the feed in each article to show? What are you going to do to enhance search engine visibility? The front pages of WordPress sites can be seen as a puzzle of posts, plugins, and widgets. You just have to find out which pieces fit best with your needs.

Save Changes   Remember to save the changes you make to your **Reading Settings**.

WordPress Discussion Settings

Default Article Settings: Pingbacks, Trackbacks, and Comments if you want notifications or comments to show in the bottom section of your posts.

Other Comment Settings: Additional comment settings can be included to help moderate content others post on your website. One of these optional settings is to require commenter's to include an email address with their comment. Even though commenters do not have to leave their REAL email – it may deter lazier folks from leaving useless comments. You can force those who want to interact with you by commenting on your posts or reading private posts and pages to register for your site. Additionally, content that is created for certain time periods can be given expiration dates, which limits users' ability to comment after an expiration date.

Email Me Whenever: As the content owner, you can be notified by email whenever there is activity on the site.

Before a Comment Appears: As the content owner you are in control of the activity on the site. You may want user comments available for publishing to site when they click enter, or you may wish to filter comments before they can be posted.

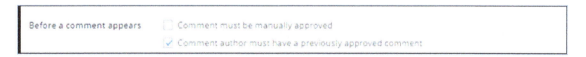

Comment Moderation: Maximize control of which comments gets held in a moderation queue.

Comment Moderation	Hold a comment in the queue if it contains 2 or more links. (A common characteristic of comment spam is a large number of hyperlinks.) When a comment contains any of these words in its content, name, URL, e-mail, or IP, it will be held in the moderation queue. One word or IP per line. It will match inside words, so "press" will match "WordPress".

Comment Blacklist: This represents a stronger way to control comments. Use this option with caution as comments that match blacklist criteria will be DELETED.

Comment Blacklist	When a comment contains any of these words in its content, name, URL, e-mail, or IP, it will be marked as spam. One word or IP per line. It will match inside words, so "press" will match "WordPress".

Avatars/Gravitars: This term refers to mini pictures that represent users on the site. WordPress uses the term Gravitars. These can be changed using plugins.

Save Changes   Remember to save the changes you make to your **Discussion Settings**.

WordPress Media Settings

The images used in your posts, pages, and galleries are controlled in the media section. WordPress allows you to make changes to the dimensions of images. Images can still be sized at the time of insert.

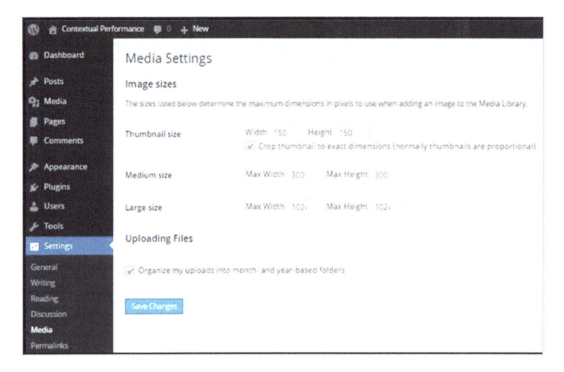

Image Sizes

Image sizes

The sizes listed below determine the maximum dimensions in pixels to use when adding an image to the Media Library.

Uploading Files

By default, WordPress creates yearly and monthly folders for images. For example: If an image is uploaded in October of 2015, it is placed into the wp-content/uploads/2015/10 folder.

Save Changes   Save any changes you make to your **Media Settings**.

Permalinks Settings

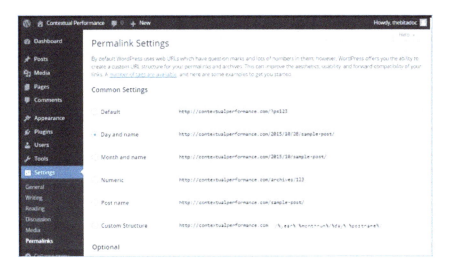

Save Changes   Save the changes you make to your **Permalinks Settings**.

Formatting WordPress Permalinks

There are many ways you can set your webpages to be viewed in the web browser URL bar.

Default: Show the number the word press application gives to the post or the page by default.

Day and name: Remembering that WordPress at its core stores pages and posts by date. The date and name folder, then the post or page name is displayed.

Month and name: The year folder, the date folder, and then the name given to the post or page is displayed.

Numeric: The folder and the number of the pages or posts are displayed.

Post name: This is the most common and recognizable choice for page and post web address because it is most similar to how native HTML web pages are displayed and is intuitive for visitors.

Custom Structure: The more advanced user may decide to create a custom URL for their posts and pages.

Optional

Save Changes   Save the changes you make to your **Permalinks** to your database.

Additionally…. You can edit an individual permalink on the post/page – underneath the title.

CUSTOMIZING THE DASHBOARD HOMEPAGE

The Dashboard Homepage Footer

This element tells you what WordPress version you're running as well as the current theme you have activated on your site.

Activity

This dashboard feature allows you to review recently published posts, highlights the most recent comments on your posts allows you to moderate those comments, and reminds you of upcoming scheduled posts.

Quick Draft Widget

The Quick Draft widget allows you to quickly and easily write a new draft, enter a post title, upload/insert media, enter post content, or add tags. Once the updates are made, click the **Publish** button or click the **Save Draft** button.

Opening and Closing Widgets

Each widget has a header bar with the widget name (left) and an open/collapse arrow (right).

STEP 1.   Click the words **At a Glance** to collapse the widget.

STEP 2.   Click the **down-pointing arrow** to reopen the widget

Drag-and-Drop Widgets

Let's drag and drop your homepage.

STEP 1.   Hover over the **Quick Draft** widget.

STEP 2.   Hold the left mouse down until it turns into a 4-headed arrow.

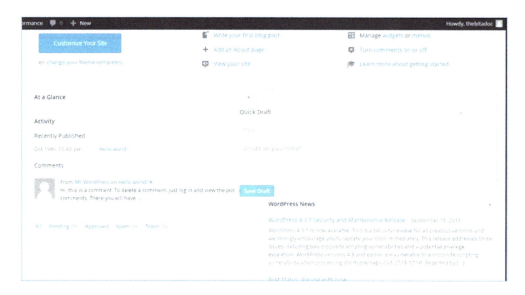

STEP 3.   Move your mouse to another area on the page and let go of the left mouse button.

Now that we are familiar with the WordPress Dashboard, let's start creating some content!

NOTES

CHAPTER SIX: CREATING CONTENT

Now that you have installed your WordPress site and gotten familiar with the elements available to create and maintain your site using the dashboard, it is time to create the content for your website using posts and pages.

In this chapter, you will:

- Create, format, and publish your first post
- Learn to manage comments and replies
- Create, format, and publish a web page
- Work with Permalinks

Content created for your WordPress site will primarily come from the posts and pages you create in the dashboard. Remember, WordPress started out as a blogging platform, so posts are essentially blog entries. Pages hold static content. Pages are favored when using WordPress to create a traditional website.

POSTS

Think of WordPress Posts as articles written for your very own newspaper. They are organized in reverse chronological order by the date they were published. The main folders are January through December, and each blog post (article) is listed by the date it was published. Like a newspaper, your posts (articles/stories) reside in sections called categories and can be tagged with words so they can be easily found. For example, sports-NFL-AFC-NFC-NY Giants.

Posts are dynamic, which means they are meant to function as a live document. Users are encouraged to interact with posts by leaving comments, liking, and sharing your information. If your posts are for information only, comment functionality can be disabled. Post types include custom and default.

Creating Your First Post

To create a new post, hoover the mouse over **Posts** in the left dashboard navigation menu and slide over and click **Add New**.

The Add New Posts Screen

The Add New Post screen is where you will create (title, compose, categorize, tag, and publish) your post. It is broken up into 7 distinct sections which are covered in detail.

The Title Textbox

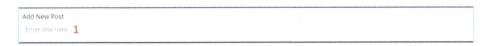

STEP 1. Locate the textbox labeled **Enter title here**.

STEP 2. Place your cursor in the textbox.

STEP 3. Type the title of your blog post.

STEP 4. Hit the **Enter** key on the keyboard.

The Post Content Text Area: In the main content area, place your cursor inside the text area and type the text of your post.

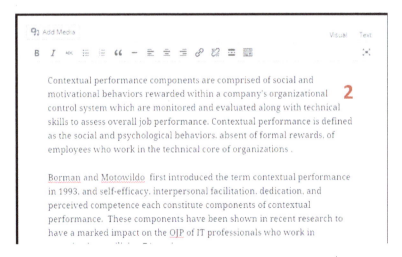

Once you have typed in some text, you will want to give it character. You can make the text in your post stand out by using the formatting elements found on the formatting toolbar. **The Formatting Toolbar** works similar to formatting toolbars in word processing programs.

The **toolbar toggle** button expands the toolbar revealing the following options:

Visual Tab: This tab displays the page content as it will appear on the web page.

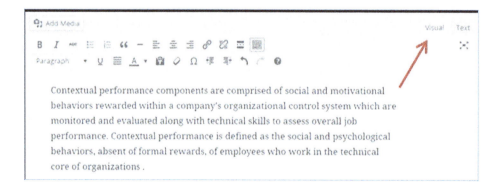

Text Tab: This tab displays the HTML code that makes up the page. It should go without saying, if you don't know html, **look but don't touch**.

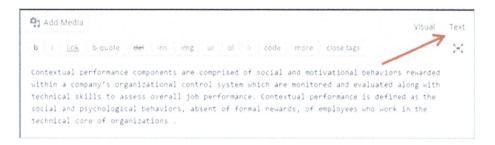

Word Count: WordPress keeps track of the words typed into the post content area.

Draft Last Saved: WordPress automatically saves the document as you work.

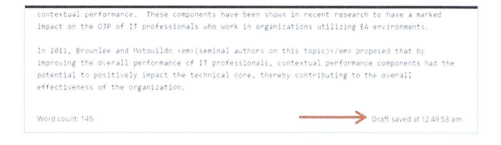

Organize Your Posts with Categories

Post Categories Section

By default, WordPress themes come with an **Uncategorized** category. You will learn how to create and configure the full Categories list in Chapter 8: *Site Organization*.

A category can easily be created from the Posts screen:

STEP 1.   Click the **+ Add New Category** link.

    Result: A text box will appear.

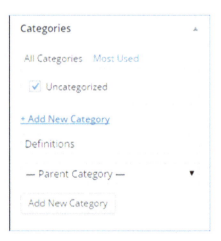

STEP 2. Type in the new Category Title.

STEP 3. Click the **Add New Category** button. Your new Category will now appear checked by default in the All Categories List.

Using Post Formats

Post Format: This is a standardized list of formats that allows you to customize how a post looks. The format types listed will depend on the formats available in the theme you are using. Remember you set the default format from Settings→Writings

Post Types

There are several different types of posts:

Aside: An aside is a small insert of information placed into a post. It is styled without a title, and it requires a plugin.

Gallery: This type of post gives you the ability to add image galleries throughout the site. Using the default WordPress gallery creator, create a gallery to your specifications and publish the post.

Link: This type of post enables you to post A link to another site. Is often used to share a link to another site by just using the site's URL. This is an advanced option.

Image: This type of post displays a single image in a Post.

Quote: A quotation is used to share information that does not hold up to the standard of being a traditional post.

Status: A status update is generally short in nature, limited to 140 characters and similar to a Twitter status update. It does not have a title and can be sent to social media sites.

Video: This type of post can refer to a single video or a video playlist to be used throughout the site.

Audio: Similarly, an audio post is an audio file or playlist to be used throughout the site.

Chat: This type of post refers to the transcript of a chat session.

Using Post Tags

Post Tags are keywords for Posts. Users will use these words to find posts in the site. Once a tag is created, it can be used for multiple posts.

To add tags to a post:

STEP 1.   Place your cursor in the Tags textbox.

STEP 2. Type the tag title.

STEP 3.   Click the **Add** button.

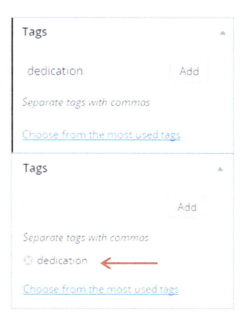

Result: The new tag will appear

STEP 4. To remove a tag, click the **Delete** button next to the tag.

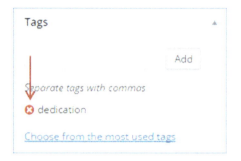

Setting a Post's Featured Image

A Post's Feature Image

The image that will be used when announcing a post is called a featured image.

To set a featured image for a post:

STEP 1.   Click the **Set featured image** link.

STEP 2.   Choose an image from the Media Library or upload a new image.

STEP 3.   Click the **Set featured image** button.

Result: The image now shows in the lower right hand corner of the Posts screen.

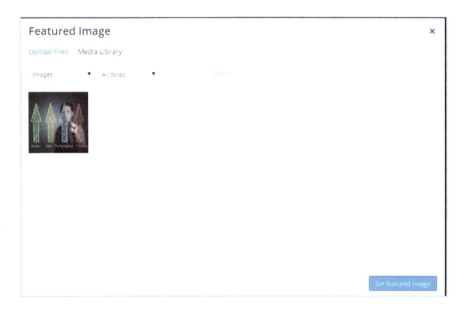

Post Screen Options

By default, the following screen options are selected.

Additional Screen Options: These options allow you to add additional functionality and elements to your posts. Screen options will vary based on the theme installed.

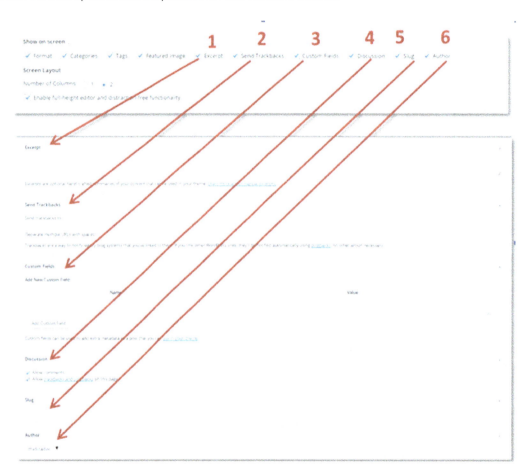

1. **Excerpt:** This is an optional summary or description of a post. WordPress generates an excerpt automatically by selecting the first 55 words of the post. You will need to use the excerpt template tag. Plugins are available to more easily administer excerpts.

2. **Send Trackbacks:** Trackbacks are a way to notify legacy blog systems that you have links in your posts to their posts.

3. **Custom Fields:** These are used to add additional meta-data to your post. They must be placed in name (key)/value pairs. Keys can be reused with different values, but the value is what shows in the meta-data listing. You will need to use the excerpt template tag. Plugins are available for easier administration of custom fields.

4. **Discussion:** Use checkmarks to determine whether you allow comments, trackbacks, or pingbacks for your post. To remove this funtionality from posts, remove the checkmark from the checkboxes.

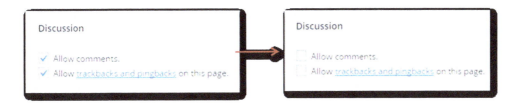

5. **Slug:** A slug is a URL-friendly version of the post or page title. It is also found on the categories screen, used when creating post categories.

6. **Author:** To choose the author of the post. Click dropdown arrow and Click the user who will be credited as the author of the post.

Publishing Posts

Once you have completed entering and formatting the post text and media, it is time to publish your post to the Internet.

Publishing and Deleting the Post

Once the development of the post is complete there are several options to consider prior to publishing the post on your site.

Draft

Draft is the status of the post prior to it being published to the web.

Save Draft Button

The save draft button is used to save the post in a draft form. Using this option will not publish the post to your site.

Preview Button

Click the **Preview** button to view the post in a browser in draft form.

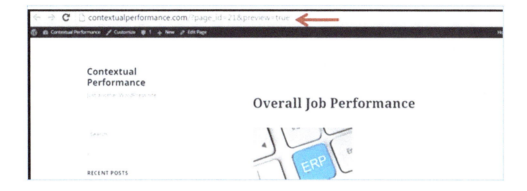

Status

- **Pending Review:** This status means that a post is waiting for administrator approval before it is published to the Web.
- **Draft:** This means a post is unpublished or under review.

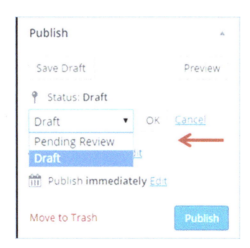

Visibility

There are 3 ways you can present posts to the world from your WordPress site.

1. **Public:** When a post is marked **Public**, anyone who visits the site can view the post.

2. **Password Protected:** For these posts, users are asked to provide a password to access the post.

   When marking a post Password Protected, you will be asked to provide a password. It is this password that you will give to users to enable them to access the post.

3. **Private:** Only registered users of the site can view posts marked **Private**.

Publish

The Publish option is used to publish the post to your site to be viewed by the world.

By default, the Publish option is set to **immediately**. To set another date and time for publishing, click the **Edit** link. **Note:** This date can be set for a future date or a date that has passed.

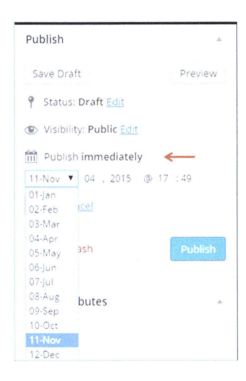
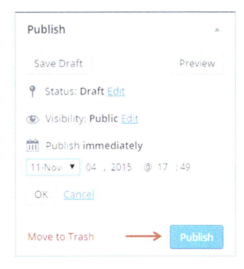

The status changes to **Published**.

Visibility is set to public.

The **Date and Time** published is recorded.

The publish button now says **Update** and the preview button now says **Preview Changes**.

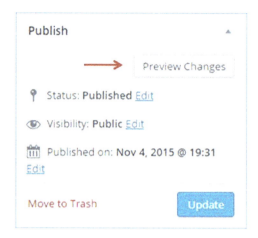

Trash

To delete the post, Click the **Move to Trash** link. This will bring up the **Confirm Navigation** popup. Click **Stay on this Page** to confirm the deletion.

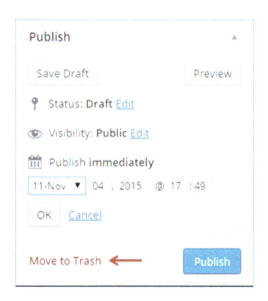

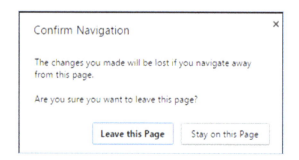

Revisions

WordPress tracks versions of the post in the revisions section of the page. Each time your post is AutoSaved, media is added, etc. you are interacting with your remote server as well as building your database. As you see the revisions section differentiates whether the post was saved automatically or saved by you.

At any time you can revisit and restore to a previous version of the post by clicking on the **Date and Time of Save** link. From the Compare Revision page you can:

STEP 1.   Return to the post editor.

STEP 2.   Compare any two revisions.

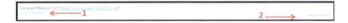

STEP 3.   Restore this Revision, or

STEP 4.   Restore this Autosave.

POST COMMENTS AND REPLIES

Managing WordPress Comments

Comments are used by site visitors to interact with a post (or a page). The Discussion setting controls comments and replies to the site. There are 2 ways to access comment settings: **Settings → Discussion.** There are also additional plugins to extend moderation functionality.

Discussion settings are global settings, meaning they are the default configurations for your site. For example, unless the settings are changed locally (on the post/page screen), visitors will hat have the ability to leave a comment unless you check the **Allow people to post comments on new articles** checkbox. It is important to work your way through the options in the Discussions Settings to reflect how you want your site to function. Take your settings for a test-drive, and remember, settings can be tweaked at any time.

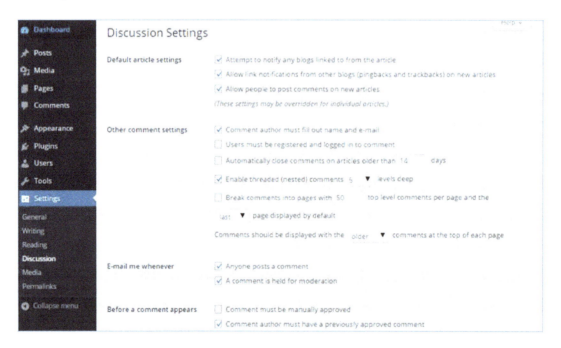

In the Discussion Section of the post (page) screen.

Allowing Comments: It is up to you whether users will be allowed to interact with a post by leaving comments.

- **In the Discussion Settings:** Place a checkmark next to **Allow people to leave comments on new articles**.

On a post-by-post basis:

- **On the Post Screen:** Place a checkmark next to **Allow comments**.
  You may have to place this option on the page by checking the discussion option in the Screen Options.

These actions will place a **Leave a Comment** link at the bottom of your post's page.

It is from here the **Leave a Reply** section will appear under your posts.

If you **DO NOT** wish to for comments to be left on any of your posts (pages), it is more time efficient to configure this in the discussion settings by taking the following actions:

In the **Discussion Settings**: Uncheck the box **Allow people to leave comments on new articles**.

On the Post Screen: Uncheck the **Allow comments** checkbox.

Configuring Comments

Configuration will determine how users interact with your site content. Configuration is a very important step in the design process. These are very specific decisions that require thought and planning. As questions like:

Do you want anyone to be able to leave a message? Do you want to place limitations on who can leave a comment? How much information do you want to know about those who are leaving comments? How long do you want your posts open for comments? Do you want to be notified when a comment is left on your website?

These are not difficult questions, and only straightforward adjustments to the Discussion Settings are required to deploy your preferences.

Moderating Comments

Allowing users and visitors to leave comments is a great way to elicit feedback from the world! It can also attract SPAMMERS as well as those whose online etiquette leaves a lot to be desired. WordPress mitigates the risk of having destructive comments on your posts by requiring a comment to be approved by an administrator prior to appearing online.

1. Do you want to read the comment prior to it showing on the post's page? Place a checkmark next to **Comment must be manually approved**.

   Do you want WordPress to remember trusted sources and automatically place their comments on the site? Place a checkmark next to **Comment author must have a previously approved comment**.

2. If you do not require a strict level of moderation, but want to be vigilant against SPAMMERS. WordPress allows you to configure your site moderation filters to look for excessive links, troublesome URLs, e-mails, IP addresses, and keywords. Remember to only place one element per line. When any of these words are found in the comment they are sent straight to comment moderation.

3. Once you isolate an offender, WordPress allows you to rid yourself of the headache by putting them on the Blacklist! Place each link, troublesome URL, e-mail address, IP addresses, and/or keyword per line in the comment Blacklist text area.

Fighting WordPress Comment SPAM

Akismet is a plugin that is installed (but not activated) in the default installation of WordPress. For more details, see **Fighting WordPress Comment SPAM with Akismet** in the Plugins section.

Managing WordPress Comment Replies

Where O Where do the comment replies go? To the comments section of course. When you have comments that require moderating, the number of comments waiting will appear at the end of the comments link in the left main navigation menu.

You will also receive an email when
Settings → Discussion:

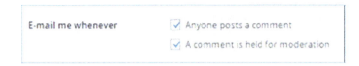

Once the user leaves their comments,
they are informed they are being held
for moderation.

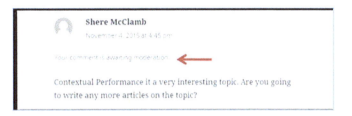

Comment moderation offers various options to work through the comments left on your site.

STEP 1. Place a checkmark next to the reply you wish to moderate.

STEP 2. The reply below is in a **Pending** status. Click the appropriate reply moderation option.

STEP 3. Choose **Approve** from the dropdown menu and click the **Apply** button.

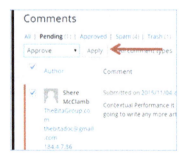

When the **Approved** option is applied, the reply is moved to an **Approved** status and is removed from the **Pending** list. The same is true if the **Spam** or **Trash** options are applied.

PAGES

Pages of your site are not considered live documents. It is here you will create content that remains static until edited. Unlike posts, you are responsible for organizing the pages in your site. Pages cannot be placed into categories, tagged, or archived. The hierarchy of your site (Parent vs. child pages) is totally up to you and is most often reflected in the main and sub menus.

Writing Page Content

To create a new post, hover the mouse over **Pages** in the left dashboard menu and slide over and click **Add New**.

The Add New Pages Screen

The Add New Page Screen is where you will create (title, page attributes, featured image, and publish) your post. It is broken up into 5 distinct sections which we will cover in detail.

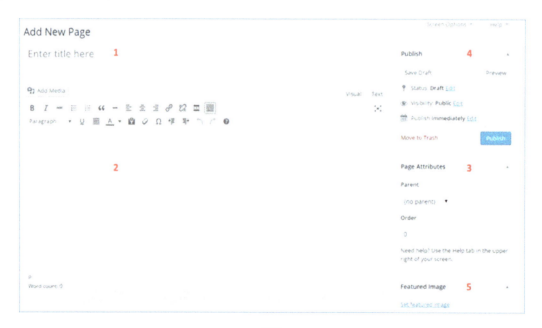

The Title Textbox

STEP 5.   **Enter title here**, is where you will place the title of the page. Place your cursor in the textbox.

STEP 6.   Type the title of your page.

STEP 7.   Hit the **Enter** key on the keyboard.

The Page Content Text Area: In the main content area, place your cursor inside the text area and type the text of your page.

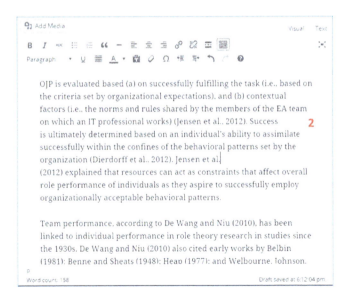

Once you have typed in some text, you will want to give it character. You can make the text in your post stand out by using the formatting elements found on the formatting toolbar.

Visual Tab: This tab displays the page content as it will be displayed on the web page.

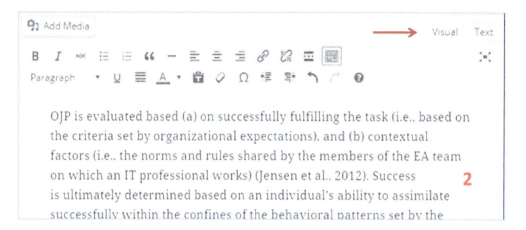

Text Tab: This tab displays the HTML code that makes up the page. It should go without saying, if you don't know html, look but don't touch.

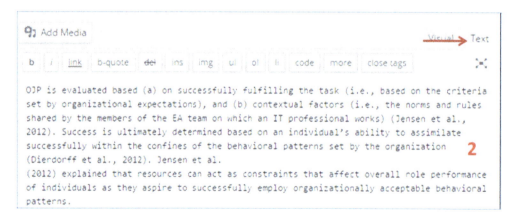

Word Count: WordPress keeps track of the words typed into the page content area.

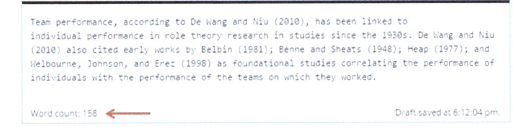

Draft Last Saved: WordPress automatically saves the document you are working on.

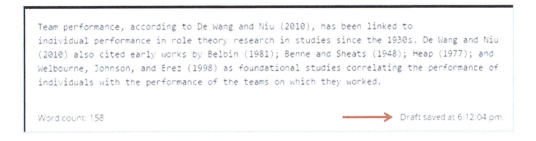

Page Attributes

WordPress pages appear on the website only when links to them are present on the site. From the Page attributes section you can configure the hierarchy of your pages and the order in which they will appear. Hierarchical layouts in WordPress are based on parent-child relationships that nest pages beneath others.

Setting the Pages Featured Image

A Page's Feature Image: The image that will be used when announcing the page is called the featured image.

To set a featured image for a page:

STEP 1.   Click the **Set featured image** link.

STEP 2.   Choose an image from the Media Library or upload a new image.

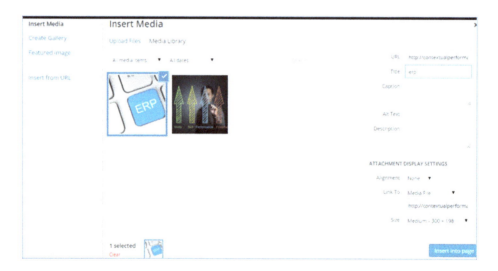

STEP 3.   Click the **Set featured image** button.

Page Screen Options

By default, the following page screen options are selected.

Additional Page Screen Options are available to add additional functionality and elements to your posts. Screen options will vary based on the theme installed.

Publishing Pages

Once you have completed entering and formatting the page text and media, it is time to publish your page to the Internet. Each time your page is AutoSaved, media is added, etc., you are interacting with your remote server as well as building your database.

Publishing and Deleting a Page

Once the development of the page is complete, there are several options to consider prior to publishing it to your site

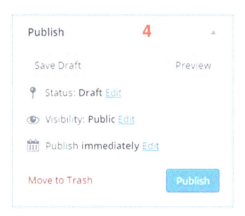

Draft

A draft is the status of the page prior to it being published to the Web.

Save Draft Button

The save draft button is used to save the page in a draft form. Using this option will not publish the page to your site.

Preview Button

Click the **Preview** button to view the page in a browser in draft form.

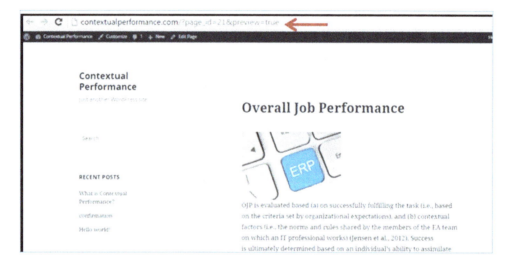

Status

A page can have 2 statuses:

- **Pending Review:** This means a page is awaiting administrator approval for publishing to the web.
- **Draft:** This means a page is unpublished and under Review

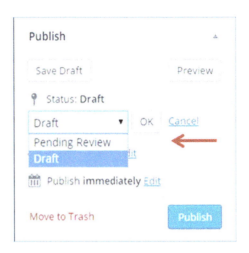

Visibility

There are 3 ways you can present pages on your WordPress site.

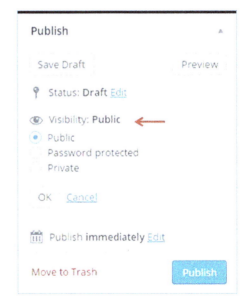

1. **Public:** When a page is marked **Public**, anyone who visits the site has access to the contents of the page.
2. **Password Protected:** For these pages, users are asked to provide a password to access the page.

   When marking a page **Password Protected**, you will be asked to provide a password. It is this password that you will give to users to enable them to access the contents of the page.

3. **Private:** Only registered users of the site can view pages marked **Private**.

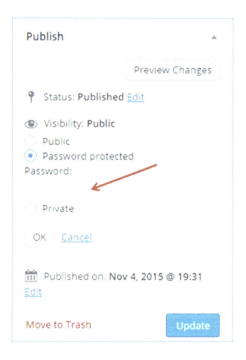

Publish

By default, the Publish option is set to publish immediately. To set another date and time for publishing, Click the **Edit** link. Note: This date can be set for a future date or a date that has passed.

Trash

To delete a page, click the **Move to Trash** link. This will bring up the *Confirm Navigation* popup. Click **Stay on this Page** to confirm the deletion.

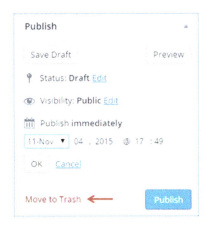 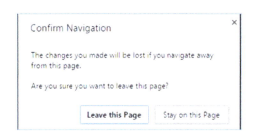

Publish

This function publishes a page to your site allowing it to be viewed by the world.

The status changes to **Published**.

Visibility is set to public.

The **Date and Time** published is recorded.

The publish button now says **Update** and the preview button now says **Preview Changes**.

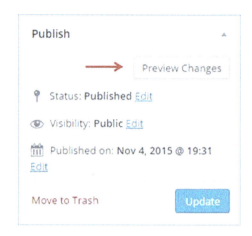

Revisions

WordPress tracks the versions of the page in the revisions section. As you see, WordPress differentiates whether the page was saved automatically or by you.

At any time, you can revisit and restore to a previous version of the page by clicking on the **Date and Time of Save** link. From the Compare Revision page you can:

STEP 1.   Return to the page editor.

STEP 2.   Compare any two revisions.

STEP 3. Restore this Revision, or

STEP 4. Restore this Autosave.

163

PERMALINKS

Modifying WordPress Permalinks

The permalink is the URL the user sees in their browser address bar. It is made from the name of the post or page. URL addresses are all lower-case and cannot contain spaces, so spaces are replaced by dashes.

To edit the Permalink:

STEP 1.   Change the name in the text box following the URL protocol of no spaces or capital letters.

STEP 2.   Click the **OK** button. The old permalink in replaced by the new one.

STEP 3.   Click the **Update** button to save these changes.

NOTES

CHAPTER SEVEN: WORKING WITH MEDIA

> *To add texture to the words in your published posts and pages, this chapter will walk you through working with the Media Library to add pictures, audio, and links. It will also teach you to build in accessibility as you create content.*

In this chapter, you will:

- Learn how to build accessibility into your site
- Learn how to navigate the Media Library
- Learn how to add images and audio to your posts and pages
- Learn how to add and remove links

Adding Media to Your Content

To add media to your posts and pages you will use the **Add Media Button** to upload and insert images, audio, video, pdfs, etc. to page and post text content.

Let's add media to our text content:

STEP 1.   Place your cursor where you want the image to be placed and click the **Add Media** button.

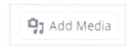

STEP 2.   Click the **Select Files** button to open the file directory on your computer where the image resides.

STEP 3.   Select an image and click **Open**.

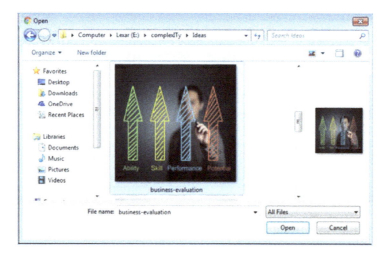

Result: The image will be uploaded to you Media Library.

Ensuring Accessibility

Accessibility refers to principals and guidelines for personal, business, and government websites that make web content such as text, images, and training materials more accessible to those with disabilities. The 508 Compliance Standards and Web Content Accessibility Guidelines WCAG are technical standards that outline the criteria for successfully developing websites that ensure accessibility for all.

Some guidelines are in line with good website design and you will comply without even realizing it. For instance, criteria for good navigation includes the ability of users navigating through a site know where they are and how to get to the information they are looking for. Users should also be able to understand site content, specifically as to the readability and characteristics of text and backgrounds.

WordPress is sensitive to these guidelines and the program has made it easier for web designers to adhere to them without coding. One example of this is that content and formatting are separated through the use of themes. The use of responsive themes allows websites to meet guidelines suggesting that sites be adaptable from one device to another. Many of the other high priority compliance guidelines pertain to the creation of tables and forms. The WordPress Media Library offers ways for website creators adhere to the guidelines to provide text alternatives for non-text elements without having to write code.

THE MEDIA LIBRARY

When viewing an image from the Media Library, you are given specific information about the image.

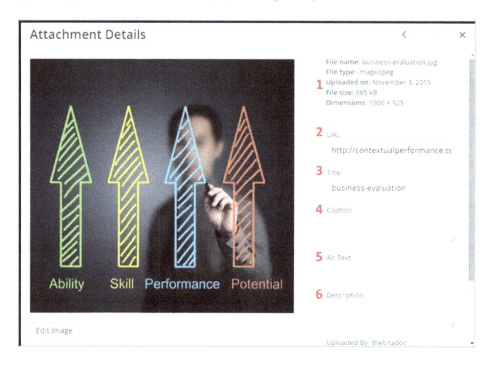

Each image in the library is saved to the year and month folder of upload. You are given the opportunity to fill in the information for each image to fulfill the criteria set for by accessibility standards for a successful website.

1. **File Information** at the time of upload.

2. **URL**

    Every media element that is uploaded to the database is given a URL that describes where it lives in your remote files. This URL, when clicked will open the image.

http://contextualperformance.com/wp-content/uploads/2015/11/business-evaluation.jpg

TOP-LEVEL DOMAIN — ON THIS DOMAIN ←

WP-CONTENT FOLDER — IS IN THIS FOLDER ←

FOLDER FOR MEDIA UPLOADS — IS IN THIS FOLDER ←

CURRENT YEAR — IS IN THIS FOLDER ←

DAY OF THE MONTH — IS IN THIS FOLDER ←

MEDIA NAME AND FORMAT

3. **Title:** The name of the file at the time it was uploaded from your computer.

4. **Caption:** Captions appear below the media element (images & video) to comply with the 508 standard requiring synchronized captions and descriptions.

5. **Alt Text:** The Alt Text describes the image and will show in its place if for some reason it does not render.

6. **Description:** The description is not visible to the user, but is read to the user by reader applications.

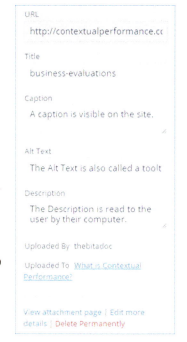

URL

http://contextualperformance.cc

Title

business-evaluations

Caption

A caption is visible on the site.

Alt Text

The Alt Text is also called a toolt

Description

The Description is read to the user by their computer.

Uploaded By thebitadoc

Uploaded To What is Contextual Performance?

View attachment page | Edit more details | Delete Permanently

ADDING AUDIO TO YOUR POSTS AND PAGES

The Media Library is the storage area for media of all types.

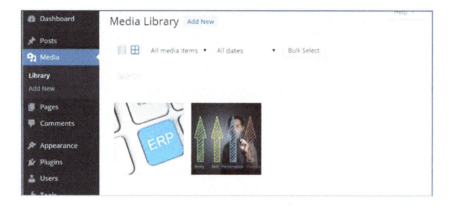

Audio files are music files in the .mp3, .wav, etc. formats. Adding audio files to your Media Library involves the same basic procedures as uploading images.

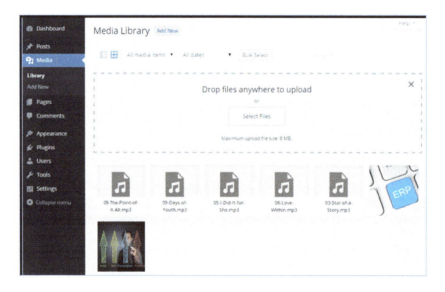

Audio, video, and image files all reside together in the order they were uploaded. WordPress provides a filter that separates the different file types for easier browsing.

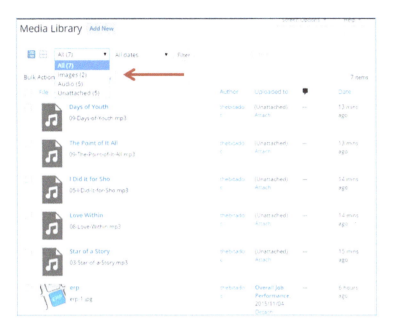

WordPress enables you to place audio files into your posts and pages. There are also free and premium plugins that offer more functionality than those listed in this section.

Audio Link (Single)

STEP 1.   Go to the Media Library and choose the audio file you want to use.

STEP 2.   Click the **Insert into Post** button.

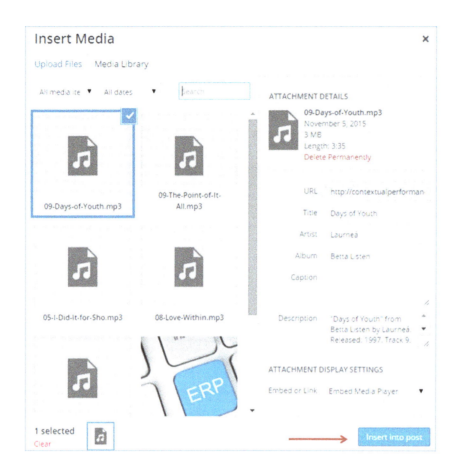

Result: The single audio file will appear on the page.

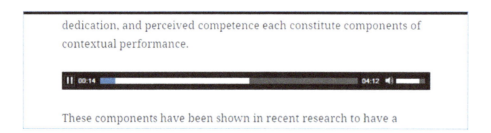

Audio Playlist

STEP 1.   Place the cursor where you would like to add the video playlist and click the **Add Media** button.

STEP 2.   Select the **Create Video Playlist** option from the Insert Media menu.

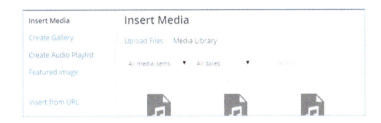

STEP 3.   Select the files you want in the playlist by clicking on them.

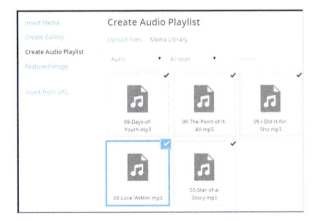

STEP 4.   Click the **Create a new playlist** button.

STEP 5.   Prepare your playlist:

- Drag and drop to order the songs, the reverse order button to...well, reverse the order of the songs.
- Configure the PLAYLIST SETTINGS by choosing whether you want to:

Show Tracklist   Show Artist in Tracklist   Show image

STEP 6. Click the **Insert Audio Playlist** button to add the playlist to your post or page.

Result: The playlist will appear on the screen.

ADDING AND REMOVING LINKS

To add a link to a page:

STEP 1.   Highlight the text you want to make a link.

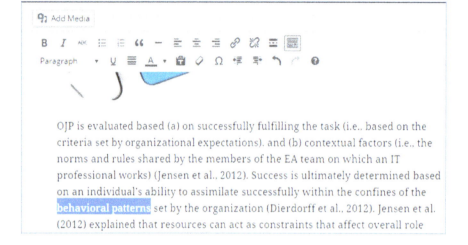

STEP 2.   Click the **Insert/Edit Link** button.

STEP 3.   Fill in the information in the Insert/Edit Link text box.

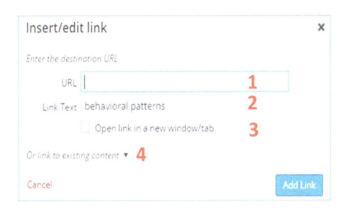

URL: This is where you want the user to end up. This should be a full URL. This link can open anything in the media library with a URL. This is a very popular way to add PDF documents to the site.

Link Text: The text you highlighted in step 1.

STEP 4.   Choose whether the new page will replace the current one or open in a new window or tab. Click the dropdown list to show the posts and pages currently saved in your site.

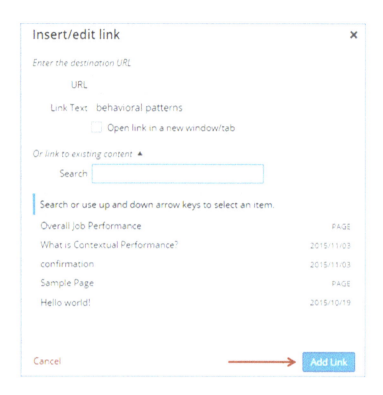

STEP 5. Type in a URL or choose one of the pages or posts and click the **Add Link** button to create the link.

> horms and rules shared by th
> professional works) (Jensen e
> on an individual's ability to a
> behavioral patterns set by the
> (2012) explained that resourc
> performance of individuals a

Result: A link of the text is created.

Removing a Link

STEP 1. Highlight the link text.

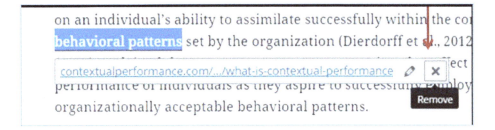

STEP 2. Click the **X** at the end of the link

NOTES

NOTES

CHAPTER EIGHT: SITE ORGANIZATION

This chapter will teach you to display your posts and pages in ways that are easy for your visitors to find and follow. You will also learn to manage your site users, registration, and logins to enhance your control as a site owner.

In this chapter, you will:

- Learn how to organize your site content with menus
- Learn how to manage users and the roles
- Learn how to add registration and login options to your site

WordPress is used by thousands to develop traditional websites. Moving visitors around your site should be carefully planned. Well-designed websites ensure that as visitors navigate a website, they always know where they are and have a clear path to get to the information they are looking for. Even though menus can contain pages, posts, and links, pages created in WordPress are only visible on the site via menus and links.

Organizing Your Pages with Menus in WordPress

The Menu screen is accessed from the **Appearance** link in the left navigation menu. Hover over Appearance and then scroll over and select **Menus** from the submenu.

The Menus screen is used to create and configure menus in WordPress regardless of the theme.

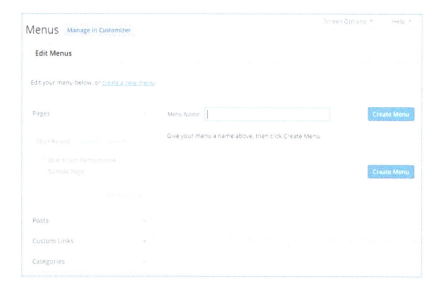

To create a menu for your site:

STEP 1.   Type the name that describes the menu in the *Menu Name* text box.

STEP 2.   Click the **Create Menu** button to create the menu.

Menu names should reflect their utility for the site. In the following examples, one intuitively knows where they will be located on a website.

- Main Menu Left
- Top Left Menu
- Top Right Menu
- Left SubMenu
- Right SubMenu
- Footer Menu

Result: The Menu is created.

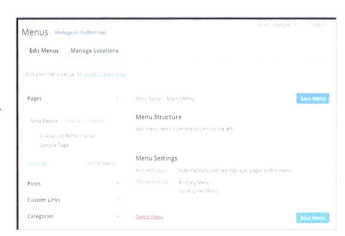

Configure Menu Settings

A Main Menu is now created, and this is the menu you will configure on this screen. You can choose to have parent pages automatically added to the menu by placing a checkmark next to **Automatically add new top-level pages to this menu** or you can build the menu manually.

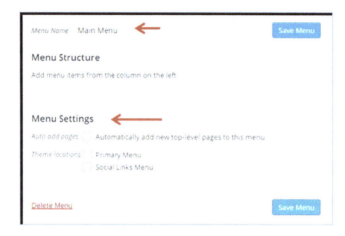

The locations available for your menu(s) are determined by the theme. This theme offers two menu locations. Because this is the main menu for the site, place a checkmark next to Primary Menu.

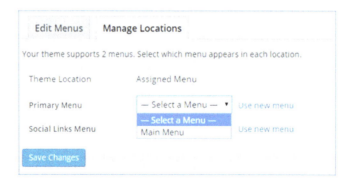

The **Manage Locations** tab gives more options as to menu locations. Here you can view all of the menus you create and place them via dropdown menus.

Adding Items to a Menu

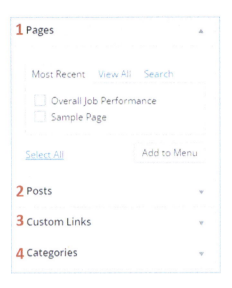

Adding Pages to the Menu

STEP 1.   Open the Pages section by Click the word **Pages** or on the **Down-Pointing Arrow**.

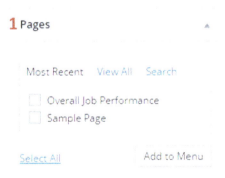

Most Recent tab: The most recently saved or updated pages in your site.

View All tab: All of the Pages in your site.

Search tab: Search for a particular page to add to the menu.

Select All link: Select all of the pages in your site.

Add to Menu button: Moves the selected page(s) to the menu.

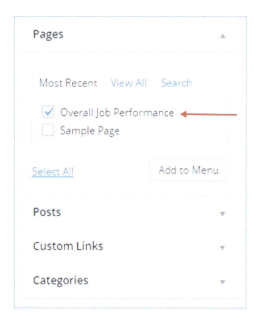

STEP 1.   Click the checkbox in front of the page you want to add to the menu.

STEP 2.   Click the **Add to Menu** button.

Result: The page is now on the menu under the Menu Structure.

Adding Posts to the Menu

STEP 1.   Open the Posts section by Click the word **Posts** or on the **Down-Pointing Arrow**.

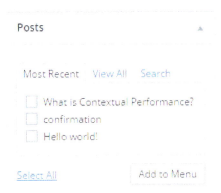

STEP 2.   Click the checkbox in front of the post you want to add to the menu.

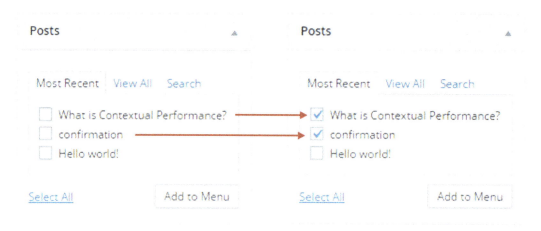

STEP 3.   Click the **Add to Menu** button.

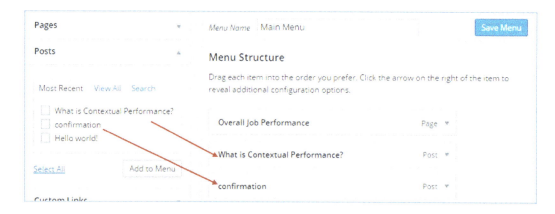

Result: The post is now on the menu under the Menu Structure.

Adding Custom URLs to the Menu

STEP 1.   Open the Custom Links section by Click **Custom Links** or on the **Down-Pointing Arrow**.

STEP 2.   Type in the full URL of the page you want the link to go to in the URL textbox. Then type in the text you want to show on the Menu in the **Link Text** textbox.

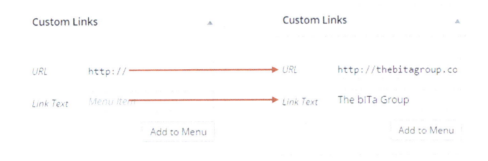

STEP 3.   Click the **Add to Menu** button.

Result: The post is now on the menu under the Menu Structure.

Saving the Menu

STEP 1. Click the **Save Menu** button to save the menu.

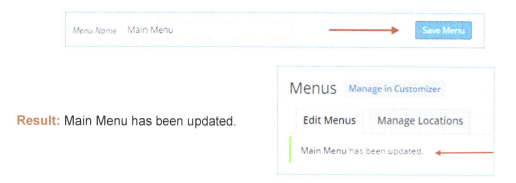

Result: Main Menu has been updated.

Creating a Hierarchical Menu

Parent Pages (Main Menu Item)

All menu items are automatically placed in the Main Menu in the parent position.

Child Pages (Submenu Item)

A child menu is commonly called a submenu. It is a list of pages that support the page it is nest under.

STEP 1.   Click the menu item that will become the child menu item.

STEP 2.   Drag and drop your way to a menu that reflects the way you want users to move around your site.

Result: The menu item is moved to the subordinate position.

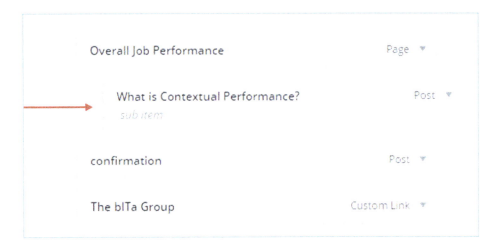

STEP 3. Click the **Save Menu** button to save the menu.

Result: Main Menu has been updated.

Place the Menu on the Website

The theme will have predetermined places.

STEP 1. Click the location where you want your menu to show on the site.

STEP 2.   Click the **Save Menu** button to save the menu.

Result: Main Menu has been saved in the Primary Menu location.

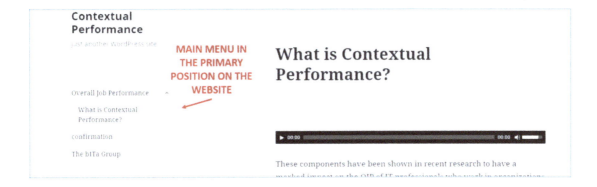

User Roles and Capabilities

Roles are used in WordPress to differentiate between individuals associated with a website. Some individuals own website content, others contribute website content, and some individuals are only able to view the content of a website.

To access User capability screens:

STEP 1.   Click the **Users** link in the Main Left Navigation.

STEP 2.   Scroll over and Click the **All Users** link.

1. **All**: This choice lists all of the users that are registered on your site.

2. **Roles**: This choice links to the users on the site by their assigned roles. It is hard to understand this looking at your new site, so let's look at a more mature site:

As you can see in this mature sample site, there are a total of 146 users who are listed by their capabilities on the site. There are 3 Administrators, 143 Subscribers, and 1 Super Administrator. Additional roles can be created, named, and added through plugins and writing functions.

There are 6 native WordPress User Roles, and their capabilities are Super Admin, Admin, Editor, Author, Contributor, and Subscriber.

Admin
ALL

Read	Delete	Del-Pub	Publish	Upload	Edit	Edit-Pub
Read	Delete	Del-Pub	Publish	Upload	Edit	Edit-Pub

Manage	Moderate	Upload	Install	Add	Install
		Import	Activate	Promote	Switch
Manage		Export	Edit	Remove	Edit
Edit			Delete	List	

Editor
Own
Private
&
Others

Read	Delete	Del-Pub	Publish	Upload	Edit	Edit-Pub
Read	Delete	Del-Pub	Publish	Upload	Edit	Edit-Pub
Manage	Moderate	Upload				

Author
Own

Read	Delete	Del-Pub	Publish	Upload	Edit	Edit-Pub

Contributor
Own

Read	Delete				Edit	

Subscriber
Own

Read

200

3. **User Checkbox**: Used to select a User. When the checkbox in front of Username is checked, all of the users will be selected.

4. **Username**: The username of the user.

5. **Name**: The User's actual name

6. **E-mail**: The User's email address

7. **Role**: The role the user is assigned on the site.

8. **Posts**: The number of posts the user has written for the site.

9. **Search Users**: Type the name of the user in the textbox and click the **Search Users** button to find a particular user.

10. **Add New** button: Click this button to add a new user to the site. You can also choose to add a new user by clicking on the **Add New** [User] in the Left Main Navigation menu.

To add a new user:

STEP 1.   Click the **Users** link in the Main Left Navigation.

STEP 2.   Scroll right and Click the **Add New** [User] link.

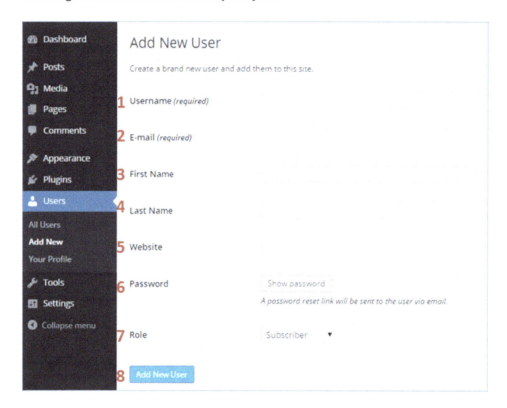

1. **Username (required)**: Users will be required to enter their username to log into the website, show as author on posts, and show as the commentor when they reply to posts.

2. **Email (required)**: Users will receive communications sent from the website at the email address listed.

3. **First Name**: The User's fist name.

4. **Last Name**: The User's last name.

5. **Website**: If the user has a website of their own, place it here. This should be a full URL that includes http://DomainName.xxx.

6. **Password**: The password the user will use to log into the website.

    STEP 1. Click the **Show Password** button.

    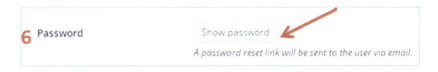

    WordPress will suggest a strong password.

    STEP 2. Choose to send this password to the user or change it. Don't worry about the password being super difficult. New users will receive a link to reset their passwords in their user notification email.

    STEP 3. Click the **Hide** button. This button is actually a toggle button depending on the state of the password.

7. **Role**: Choose which role the user will occupy on the site. If necessary, refer to the capabilities chart.

8. **Add New User [button]**: Click this button to submit the new user information to your database.

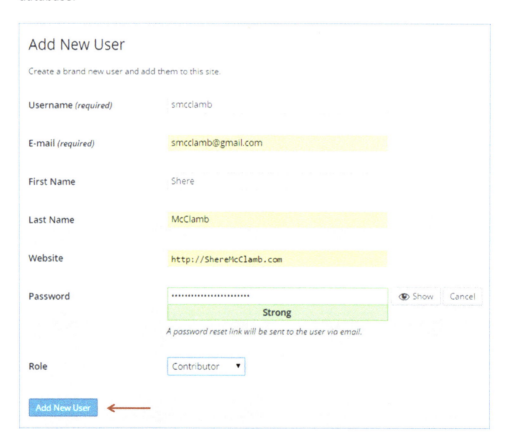

Three things will happen once you click the **Add New User** button:

1. The new user will show on the User List.

2. The Admin(s) will receive an email that a new user has been registered on the site.

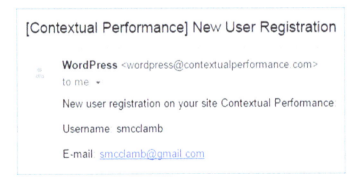

3. The new user will receive an email.

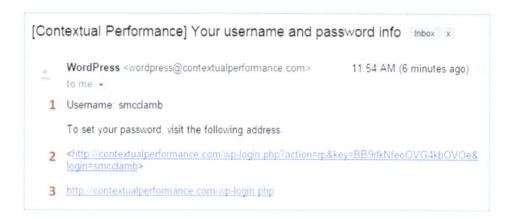

This email will give the newly registered user the information they need to get started as a user on the website.

- Their Username.
- The change password link. When the user clicks on this link from their email, they will be taken to a login screen with the default email address you sent from the add new user screen.

1. They can make their personal preference changes to their password.

2. Click the **Reset Password** button.

- The user will click the link to access the login page of your site. You will also use this link on your site for users to log in at their convenience .

1. The user will type in their **Username**.
2. The user will type in their **Password**.
3. They will have the option to check the **Remember Me** checkbox if it is a personal device that only they will have access to.
4. The user will Click the **Log In** button to access the site.
5. If the user needs to retrieve thieir password, they should Click the **Lost your password** link.
6. The **Back to [Website Name]** link will take users to the main page of the site.

To view and update your Profile (These steps refer to Admin as well as currently logged in users):

STEP 1.   Click the **Users** link in the Left Main Navigation.

STEP 2.   [Admins Only] Scroll over and Click the **Your Profile** link.

The Left Main Navigation displays links and capabilities based on the user role of the individual currently logged into the site.

Make any necessary changes and click the **Update Profile** button.

Adding Register and Login Options to your Site

Most WordPress themes are configured with user registration and login links as defaults.

Samples:

Add a registration link to your site:

First you will need to allow users to register to your site:

STEP 1.   Go to the **Settings** link in the Left Main Navigation menu.

STEP 2.   Check **Anyone can register**.

STEP 3.   Choose their role from the **New User Default Role** list.

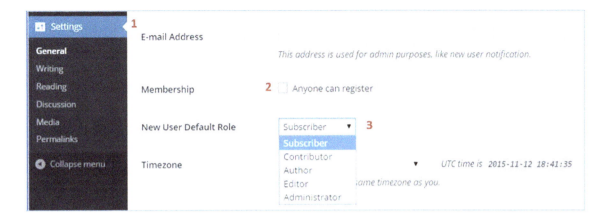

STEP 4.   Click the **Save Changes** button to save your update.

Result: The Register option will appear on your site.

Note: You can also install plugins to add functionality to the user registration process. For example, certain plugins allow you to approve any user prior to their completing the registration process.

Add a registration link to your site:

STEP 1.   Add the following link to your site: http://YourWebiteFullDomainURL/user-registration/

Result: The user will be taken to the default registration screen.

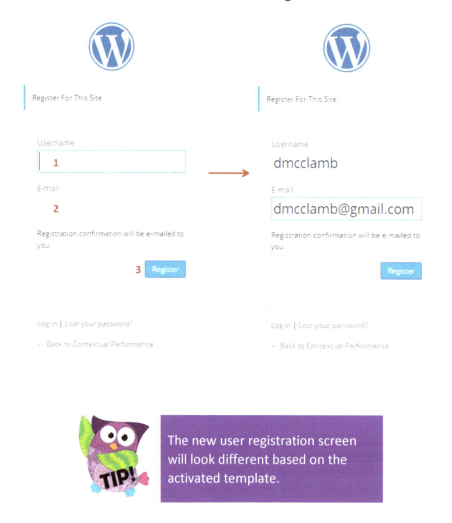

The new user registration screen will look different based on the activated template.

The User will:

STEP 1.   Fill in the **Username** field.

STEP 2.   Fill in the **E-mail** field.

STEP 3.   Click the **Register** button.

Result: The new user will receive the message: Registration complete. Please check your email. This is the same process as adding a new user from the dashboard.

Add a login link to your site:

Add the following link to your site: http://FullWebsiteDomainURL/log-in.php/

Result: The user will be taken to your site's login screen.

NOTES

NOTES

CHAPTER NINE: EXTENDING WORDPRESS BEHAVIORS

In this chapter you will learn to extend the functionality of your site so that it is interesting as well as informative. The use of themes, plugins, and widgets is covered in this chapter.

In this chapter, you will:

- Learn how to locate, download, install, activate, configure, and delete plugins
- Learn how to locate, download, install, activate, configure, and delete widgets
- Learn how to locate, download, install, activate, and configure site themes

Now that we have WordPress installed and have concept of how to administer the basics of the site, it is time to extend the functionality of the site by adding some bells and whistles. Plugins and widgets are used to add special functionality.

PLUGINS

What is a Plugin?

You can add additional functionality to your WordPress site by finding, downloading, installing, activating, and configuring plugins. A plugin is user-friendly software that is written by developers for you to use on your WordPress site. Configuration for these software elements range from very easy to quite difficult. Just as with anything free, plugins range from great to downright miserable. It is important to note that most free plugins do not come with technical support if you run into problems.

Finding and Downloading a Plugin

Many of the plugins you will want for your website can be found in the Plugins section of the WordPress Codex. A great place to start when searching for plugins to add functionality to your site is the Official WordPress Plugins Repository (https://wordpress.org/plugins/).

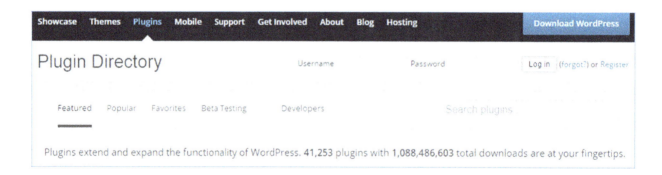

Searching for a plugin on the WordPress.org website:

STEP 1.   Go to the WordPress repository.

STEP 2.   Type the functionality you want for your site in the search text box and hit enter. This may take some tweaking to get the search results you desire.

The Search Results Page

1. A Search Results link is now displayed on the plugins main menu.

2. The total number of plugins that were found using the search criteria.

3. Page navigation of the search results when the keyword calendar was entered into the search bar.

4. The descriptions and links to the plugins found that met the search criteria.

The Anatomy of a Plugin Search Result

Not all plugins will be compatible with the version of WordPress you have installed. Make sure you check this prior to installing it on your site.

1. **Plugin Image**: An icon for the plugin.

2. **Plugin Name**: The name the plugin is known by. Also the name that can be used in a search.

3. **Plugin Description**: A concise description of the functionality the plugin will give to your site.

4. **Plugin Author**: The developer or developers who coded the plugin in php.

5. **Plugin Rating Average**: WordPress users rate a plugin using a 5-star rating system.

6. **Number of Active Installs**: The number of WordPress sites that use this plugin.

7. **Last Updated**: A plugin that is kept up-to-date by the developer is usually more dependable and has fewer unresolved issues.

8. **WordPress Version Compatibility**: The version of WordPress the plugin was developed to be used with.

Viewing a Plugin on the WordPress.org Website

Click the **Plugin Title** link.

Result: You will be taken to the Plugin's main page.

1. Plugin **Name**

2. **Short Description**: The same description from the main screen.

3. **Download Button**: Click this button to download the zipped file to install on your site.

4. **Plugin Description Tab**: A detailed description of the plugin.

5. **Plugin Installation Tab**: Directions on how to install the plugin.

6. **Screenshots** of the plugin at work.

7. **A Log** of the changes, updates, versions, and upgrades to the plugin.

8. **Stats**: History of downloads.

9. **Support**: User and developer posts and replies.

10. **Reviews**: The star rating page.

11. **Developer Information**: Information the developer has shared.

Installing Plugins from the Dashboard of Your Site

STEP 1.   Hover over the **Plugins** link in the Left Main Navigation and then move your mouse over to **Add New**.

Result: The Add Plugins page opens.

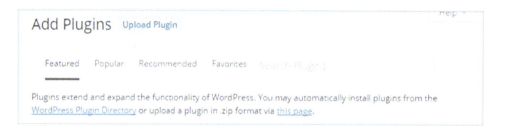

STEP 2.   Search for the plugin that matches your criteria.

STEP 3.   Choose a plugin and click the **Install Now** button on the plugin ad.

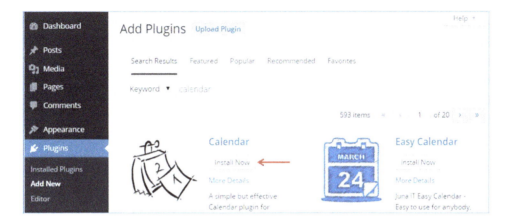

Result: The plugin installation runs.

1. Download the plugin into the site plugin directory.

2. Unpack the downloaded zipped file.

3. Install the plugin

4. Receive a successful installation message!

Make sure the plugin you choose is compatible to the version of WordPress you have installed. If not you will receive an error message.

Successful installation of the plugin simply means that when you are ready to use this functionality you can **Activate** and **Configure** it. A Plugin can sit installed but unactivated in the plugins section of your site.

Activating and Configuring Plugins

Once a Plugin is installed, it will show on the **Installed Plugins** list.

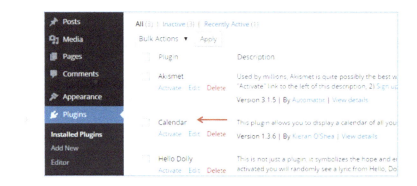

STEP 1. Click the **Activate** link.

Result: The **Activate** and **Delete** links disappear from the options, and a **Deactivate** link appears.

Calendar — This plugin allows you to display a calendar of all your even
Deactivate   Edit   Version 1.3.6 | By Kieran O'Shea | View details

224

Find where on the Left Main Navigation the plugin resides. Plugins will reside in different places on the Left Main Navigation based on their functionality. A plugin will reside:

As a link on the Left Main Navigation

Example:

Under the Settings link

Example:

Configuring a Plugin

Configuring or updating the settings for your site will sometimes will sometimes be accomplished through the Installed Plugins page. However, most of the time, option links for settings can be found on the Left Navigation Menu.

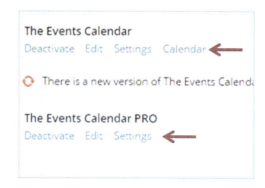

STEP 1.   Hover over or Click the name of the plugin where it resides to view its configuration options.

Some plugins will let you know that configuration or set-up is required.

Warning: Calendar setup incomplete. Go to the calendar plugin settings to complete setup.

STEP 2.   Click each of the option links and set the plugin up according to your site's needs.

Managing (Updating and Upgrading) Plugins

Updating a Plugin

As explained earlier, you want to install plugins with a good reputation (a solid track record of interaction with the community, updates, and upgrades). When a plugin requires updating, an alert will show in the Main Left Navigation to the right of the plugins link.

STEP 1.   Go to the **Installed Plugins** page to find the plugins that require updating. There is often a message at the top of the page letting you know which plugin needs attention.

The last line on the plugin in the list will state what needs to be done.

🔄 There is a new version of Cool fade popup available. View version 8.7 details or update now.

STEP 2.   Click **update now**. The plugin update may or may not require additional information from you.

Pay close attention to all messages during plugin updates. You may also receive a warning concerning the information currently controlled by the plugin.

Result: Updated replaces the needs updating message,

🔄 There is a new version of Cool fade popup available. View version 8.7 details or update now.   ➡   ✓ Updated!

Upgrading a Plugin

Many plugins are completely free to use with your WordPress site. Premium plugins are (developer tagged) top-of-the-line plugins that have to be purchased prior to downloading or installation. Other plugins limit functionality on the free version but offer more options for a fee. Developers will not necessarily tell you up front that you are installing the free version of a full-version-for-a-fee plugin.

228

The way in which you upgrade a plugin is up to the developer and there are too many possibilities to cover them all here.

Donating to the Developer

Even though there are thousands of free plugins to use and enjoy, if you use a free plugin, you should consider donating to the developer for their efforts. Developers who donate their time and expertise to create free plugins play an important role in making your site awesome. There is usually a link for donations when downloading a plugin.

Deactivating and Deleting a Plugin

It is very common for an Admin to choose, download, install, and start to configure a promising plugin, only to find out it does not fit the needs of the site. There are two options for removing the functionality of a plugin from your website.

The first is to deactivate the plugin. Deactivating a plugin removes the links from the menu and the plugin's functionality from your site. With this option, the plugin remains on the Installed Plugins list and it is still saved in your remote files. You can re-activate the plugin in the future without having to find, download, and install it again.

Click the **Deactivate** link to deactivate a plugin.

The second option is to delete the plugin. Deleting a plugin completely removes the plugin from your site and site files.

STEP 1. Click the **Delete** link underneath the plugin name.

Result: The Delete Plugin screen appears.

1. A warning screen appears informing you that you are about to remove the plugin.
2. The warning screen shows the name of the plugin that is being removed.
    There are two decision buttons:
3. Yes, Delete
4. No, Take Me Back
5. Click this link to view all of the files associated with this plugin also deleted with this action.

STEP 2.   Click the **Yes, delete these files** button.

Result: The plugin is permanently deleted and removed from the Installed Plugins list.

Fighting WordPress Comment SPAM with the Akismet Plugin

Akismet is a plugin that is installed (but not activated) in the default installation of WordPress. According to the WordPress Codex, Akismet uses a unique algorithm combined with a community-created database to 'learn' which comments are comment spam and which are legitimate.

STEP 1.   Click the **Activate** link.

STEP 2.   Click the **Activate your Akismet account** button.

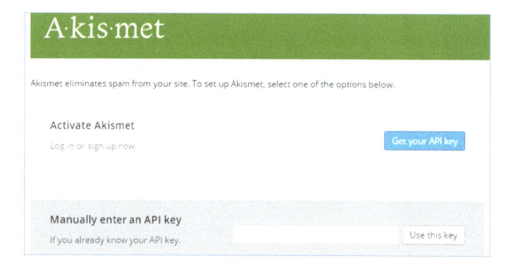

STEP 3.   Click the **Get your API key** button.

Result: You will be taken to the Akismet website to complete the registration process.

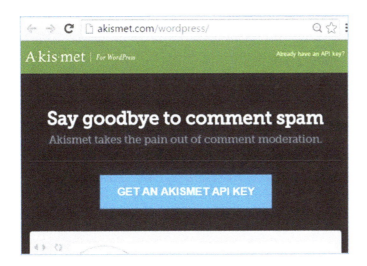

 If you choose not to activate the Akismet plugin, there are many other free and premium SPAM-fighting plugins available.

WORDPRESS WIDGETS

What is a Widget?

A widget is no-code function block that provides functionality to sections of your website. It is helpful to think of plugins and widgets as puzzle pieces that combine to create the site you desire. Widgets most commonly appear on the homepage in the header, sidebars, and footer sections of a WordPress site. Widgets include functionality such as a calendar, custom menus, advertising areas, search, social media, and news scrolls to name just a few. Some plugin functionalities are deployed through widgets or have a widget option.

Working with Widgets

To access the widget area:

STEP 1.   Hover over or click the **Appearance** link and then scroll over to and click **Widgets** in the Left Main Navigation menu.

Result: The Widget Area opens.

This is an extremely simple version of a widget area, to give you a more realistic view of widget areas, here are a few examples:

Example 1:

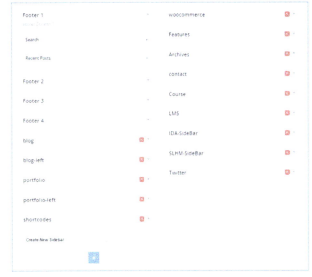

Example 2:

Home Page Widget 1		Sidebar 10	
Cool fade popup		Sidebar 11	
		Sidebar 12	
Home Page Widget 2		Sidebar 13	
Home Page Widget 3			
		Sidebar 14	
Home Page Widget 4		Sidebar 15	
Home Page Widget 5			
		Sidebar 16	
Home Page Widget 6		Sidebar 17	
Tabpanel widget			
		Sidebar 18	
Home Sidebar		Sidebar 19	
Blog Sidebar			
		Sidebar 20	
Sidebar 1		Footer Column 1	
Sidebar 2			
		Footer Column 2	
Sidebar 3		Footer Column 3	
Sidebar 4			
		Footer Column 4	
Sidebar 5		Footer Column 5	
Sidebar 6			
		Home Page Widget X	
Sidebar 7			
Sidebar 8			

The Widget Area

Creating widgets is a process of expanding and adding functionality by configuring the widget blocks.

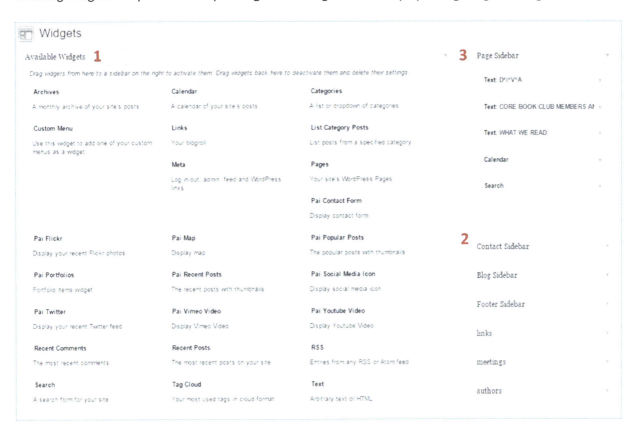

1. **Available Widgets**: The functionality that is available to place in widget areas either comes as a default with the theme or will be installed by the site owner. Each theme differs in the functionality that is preinstalled. This is one of the decision points when shopping for the right theme for your website. Available functionality is located on the left side of every widget area. The names of the widgets is the same as the plugin that was downloaded.

2. **Widget Areas**: A widget area may be predefined. Most themes will come with predefined widget areas (contact, blog, footer, and page sidebars).

3. **Configuring the Widget**: Widgets are built by using and configuring the function code blocks from the left side of the widget area.

Configuring a Widget

Expanding, Collapsing, and Rearranging Widgets:

Each widget can be expanded or contracted by clicking on the widget title bar.

STEP 1.   Click the down-pointing arrow on the widget title bar.

Result: The widget is expanded revealing configuration details.

STEP 2.   Fill in the configuration details.

STEP 3.   Click the **Save** button.

STEP 4.   Close the widget by clicking on the **Close** link.

Result: The widget is configured and closed.

STEP 5. Go to the website and view the widget on the site.

Downloading a WordPress Widget

Additional functionality using widgets can be used by installing a widgetized plugin.

STEP 1. Go to Add New plugins on the left main navigation menu.

STEP 2. Search for widgets

STEP 3.   Choose and install the plugin that contains the widget you want to use on your site.

STEP 4.   Activate the plugin by clicking on the **Activate** button.

Result: the plugin is now listed in the Installed Widget list.

STEP 5. Go to widget area and locate the widget.

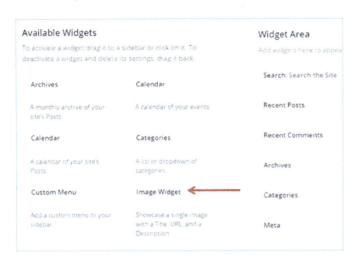

STEP 6. Create a widget area by dragging the Available Widget and dropping it in the widget area.

Result: The widget now resides in the widget area and is ready to be configured.

STEP 7.   Configure the widget.

STEP 8.   Save your settings by clicking on the **Save** button.

STEP 9.   Click the **Close** link to close the widget.

Result: The widget area appears in the widget area and on the website.

STEP 10.   Go to the website homepage to view your update.

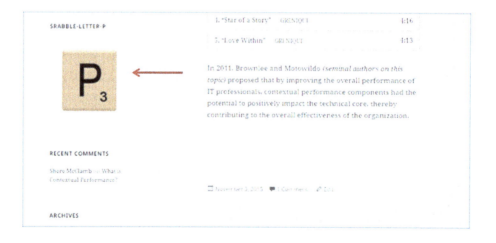

Customizing the WordPress Widget Screen

Widgets can be moved up or down or from column to column by using the drag-and-drop method. Hover the mouse cursor over the widget title bar. When the mouse cursor changes to a 4-arrow, hold the left-mouse button down, drag the widget to where you want to place it, and then release the mouse button.

Disabling and Removing a Widget

Widgets can be removed from the site by removing or deleting it or on the plugin level by deactivating or deleting the plugin.

A widget can be removed from the active widgets area and the widget area on the site where it resides while retaining the configuration settings.

To remove the widget, but retain configuration settings:

STEP 1.   Click the Header bar of the widget you want to remove.

STEP 2.   Drag it to the **Inactive Widgets** area.

Result: The widget is removed from the active widget area and the homepage.

A widget can be removed from the active widgets area and the widget area on the site where it resides. This option will delete the configuration settings, but the widget will remain in the available widgets area.

To remove a widget and delete its configuration settings:

STEP 1. Open the widget.

STEP 2. Click the Delete link.

Result: The widget is removed from the widget area, the configuration settings are deleted, but the widget still resides in the available widgets area.

To completely remove a widget from the site, follow the instructions for deleting a plugin.

THEMES

Themes are the foundation of the WordPress site layout. The use of themes is one of the elements that makes WordPress so user-friendly. Choosing a theme that conveys the look and feel you are trying to convey is vital. Taking the time to search for and choose the right theme is a major step in planning your site. There are literally thousands of themes to choose from. In your search you will find a wide range of theme choices. There are simple layouts with few widget areas and plenty of white-space. There are layouts created for photographers and artist waiting for lots of pictures. Bloggers often have magazine-type layouts to handle lots of information. Depending on the purpose of your site, you will have a wide range of options to choose from. Price may also be a consideration. WordPress themes range in price-point from free to premium. Again, how much you spend on a theme will depend on your goals for your site.

FINDING THE RIGHT THEME

Locating the right theme for your site is done simply by searching. A search using key words such as free WordPress theme, premium WordPress theme, or top 10 WordPress themes will net some really good leads. There are also blogs that regularly review and rank WordPress themes, theme sites, and theme authors.

WordPress › Popular « Free WordPress Themes
https://wordpress.org/themes/browse/popular/ ▾ WordPress ▾
Search WordPress.org for: Showcase. Themes. Plugins. Mobile. Support ...
Featured. Popular. Latest. Feature Filter. Search Themes. Apply Filters Clear.

50+ Best Free Responsive WordPress Themes 2015 - Colorlib
https://colorlib.com/wp/free-wordpress-themes/ ▾
Sep 20, 2015 - However, quality free WordPress themes are not easy to find that is why I decided to gather some of the finest free WordPress themes on hand.
eCommerce - Advertise on Colorlib - Portfolio

Free WordPress Themes at WordPress.com
https://theme.wordpress.com/themes/sort/free/ ▾
Discover Free WordPress Themes on the WordPress.com Theme Showcase. Here you can browse and search all WordPress themes available on ...

The 40 best free WordPress themes - Creative Bloq
www.creativebloq.com/web-design/free-wordpress-themes-712429 ▾
Jul 3, 2015 - In this article we've selected some of the very best free WordPress themes for you to use in your projects. Each is not only free to use and open ...

Choosing the Right One for Your Website

Understanding website design fundamentals is essential when determining whether a theme is right for your site. Take the time to ask some fundamental website design questions prior to looking for a theme.

- What is the goal of my website?
- Who is my audience?
- What messages am I attempting to convey?
- What look and feel do I want for my site?
- Do I require a picture-laden or text-heavy layout?

WordPress should be used as a tool to present your website to the world, not a shortcut from the real work it takes to design, create, and maintain a site.

Editing Themes to Make Them Your Own

As we saw, you can use pages, posts, images, plugins, and widgets to make a WordPress website come to life. Most themes are also responsive and optimized for mobile devices. Most premium themes come with many choices that include multiple layouts and homepages with image sliders, custom widget sets, font choices, unlimited sidebars, SEO capabilities, and multiple translations ready to be deployed without coding knowledge.

Installing a New Theme through the WordPress Dashboard

Changing the appearance of your site by swapping out one theme for another in WordPress can be completed with a few clicks.

STEP 1.   Click **Appearance** in the Left Main Navigation and then Click the **Themes** link.

Result: The Themes Screen appears.

STEP 2. Click the **Add New** button between the themes header and the themes search bar.

Result: 1. The themes headers turns into **Add Themes**.

2. A button to **Upload a Theme** appears.

3. 15 featured themes are shown.

STEP 3. Choose a theme to replace the current theme. You can view more information about each of the themes by hovering you mouse over and clicking on them. Click **Details & Preview.**

Result: You are taken to the Preview Page for the theme.

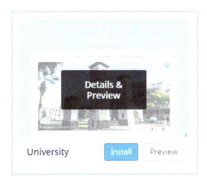

STEP 4.   To install the theme (replacing your current theme), Click the **Install** button in the top left.

Result: The Plugin Installation Runs.

1. Downloading the theme into the site theme directory.

2. Unpacking the downloaded zipped file.

3. Installation of the theme.

4. Successful theme installation message!

5. WordPress gives an opportunity to view your website with the new theme by clicking on the **Live Preview** link.

1. If you like the changes you can **Save and Activate** the theme from this screen.

2. If you would like to view other themes, click the **Change** button.

3. Once you have previewed the theme
   and you like how it looks, you can
   replace the current theme by clicking
   on the **Theme Activate** link.

4. If you do not approve of how the
   theme looks, you can choose to keep
   the current theme by clicking on the
   Return to Theme Installer link.

Installing a Theme from a Zipped File

STEP 1.   First you will need to download the zipped file that contains the new theme to your local file folder.

 Unzip the theme and review the files inside. Many theme developers nest the actual **theme** inside the main theme folder that also contains instructions and other files you need to properly install and maintain the theme.

Once you have the zipped theme files saved locally.

STEP 2.   Click **Appearance** in the Left Main Navigation and then Click the **Themes** link.

 Make sure the theme is compatible to the version of WordPress you have installed. If not you will receive an error message here.

Result: The Themes Screen appears.

256

STEP 3.   Click the **Add New** button between the themes header and the themes search bar.

Result: The themes header turns into **Add Themes** and a button to **Upload a Theme** appears.

STEP 4.   Click the **Upload Theme** button between the themes header and the themes search bar.

STEP 5.   Click the **Choose File** button and choose the zipped file.

STEP 6.   Click the **Install Now** button.

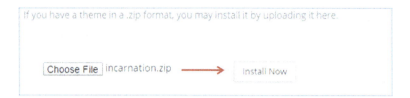

Result: The plugin installation runs. Follow the installation instructions to complete the installation of the theme.

NOTES

CHAPTER TEN: SITE MAINTENANCE

Working through chapters 1 through 9 should have allowed you to create a basic website that can accommodate your material. This chapter focuses on maintenance activities to keep your site updated and functional.

In this chapter, you will:

- Learn how to back up your site's database
- Learn how to back up your site files
- Learn how to update themes, plugins, and widgets using the dashboard
- Learn the importance of updating outdated content

The ongoing maintenance of your site is just as important as getting your site up and running. Instituting a strong and regular backup schedule is one of the most important tools you can deploy for the health of your site. Remember, WordPress and most of the themes and plugins you will use are constantly being updated and new versions are rolled out daily. Maintaining all of the elements it took for you to build the site is key to keeping your site in tip-top shape for years to come.

Backing up the Database

The database you created to hold the content of your site is the brains of your operation. Protecting the database from being corrupted or deleted is very important. It is also very important to back your database up before you make any major changes, updates, or upgrades to your site. It is good practice to keep a version of your database on external drive like a jump drive.

Backup Methods

It is a smart move to use plugins to back up your database regularly. The most common ways to back up a WordPress site database are through plugins. There are numerous plugins that can perform a thorough backup of your database. The keywords **database backup** typed into the plugins search textbox yielded 439 plugins that met that criteria.

Backing up your Site Files

The files that make up your website are also vulnerable and must be protected and backed up regularly. Using the FTP client (Filezilla), most updated files from your server can be downloaded and saved locally.

UPDATING THE SITE THROUGH THE DASHBOARD

The WordPress Dashboard relays reminders when elements of your website require updating and upgrading. The first reminder of updates is the circle reminder next to the **Updates** link at the top of the Left Main Navigation. This number is a combination of all of the updates needed to get the site up-to-date.

WordPress Versions

The WordPress application is a living application that is being improved regularly through version updates. When a new version of WordPress is available, a message will appear in the Dashboard stating a [new] version number is available.

To view the particulars of the update, Click the hypertext link **WordPress x.x.x**. You will be taken to the version page of the update on the WordPress.org site.

To update the WordPress version running your site, Click the **Please update now** link. You will be presented with the choice to either automatically update your site by clicking the **Update Now** button or download the zipped file of the update to your local folder. For most, using the **Update Now** button will work just fine to update the site. For those individuals whose site files are nested deeper in their remote host folders hierarchy, downloading the zipped update file and using the FTP client to update the WordPress files and folders would be a better approach.

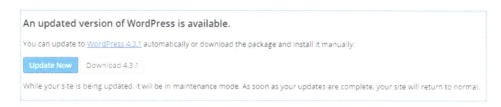

Once WordPress detects the update in the application, the Admin of the site will receive an email notifying them when:

1. The new version of WordPress has been updated.
2. Any further action is required of the Admin Role for this update.
3. Links to support for the update are available at WordPress.org.
4. Any plugins, themes, etc. require updating.

Comments

 When there are comments (replies to Posts and Pages) that have not been moderated, a reminder of the number of comments that require attention will appear in the reminder bubble in the Left Main Navigation.

Plugins

 When there are installed Plugins that require updating or upgrading, WordPress reminds the Admin in a number of ways. The first is to place a reminder bubble in the Left Main Navigation with the number of plugins that require attention.

A reminder in the the main area of the Dashboard will show reminders at the top of each page that there are Plugins that require updating. Each of the Plugins can receive the attention they require by Click the **Update Plugins** button. WordPress will work through each of the Plugins until they are all updated.

When the Admin is on the **Installed Plugins** screen, a red bar with an update message will appear in any Plugin that requires attention. The attention line will describe what needs to be done to bring the Plugin up-to-date.

Themes

Developers are continuously working to make their themes better, so when there is a release to update your theme, the Admin will receive a reminder message in the Dashboard that new versions of installed themes are available. Be sure to read and act on any and all information on warnings and updates prior to clicking on the **Update Themes** button.

Themes

The following themes have new versions available. Check the ones you want to update and then click "Update Themes".

Please Note: Any customizations you have made to theme files will be lost. Please consider using child themes for modifications.

Update Themes

Outdated Content

Periodically the content of a website should be reviewed for outdated information. Outdated information is different from dated information. One would expect to find a history of posts on a mature blog, and this is considered dated material. However, outdated material refers to information that is no longer valid. Outdated material should be updated or removed.

Old Media

Many more pictures, music, and videos are uploaded than are required or used on a website. Periodically, the Media Library should be reviewed and purged of media that will no longer be used on the site. This is important as the size of media elements increases the size of the site folders and may affect the price you pay for file space to your host.

Broken Links

Broken links occur over time, and they can be damaging to a website's reputation. Combing through pages of a site to find broken links can be time consuming and cumbersome. The use of plugins to search the pages and posts of the site to search for broken links is a smarter way to handle this task.

When the key term broken links is used to search through the plugin directory, 790 results were returned that met that criteria. Once the links are identified, then they can be fixed or updated.

INSTALLING WORDPRESS LOCALLY

It is also possible to install the WordPress software on your local computer. A local install is a great way to practice in a safe environment that lets you try out new themes, plugins, etc. without jeopardizing your public-facing website.

Replacing the LAMP Stack

The same technologies are required when running WordPress on a local computer. The difference is that all of the technologies and files will reside on your computer. The LAMP stack will be replaced with a WAMP server. Wampserver is available for free under the GPL license as WordPress, Notepad++, and Filezilla. Please Note: Wampserver 2.5 is incompatible with Windows XP, SP3, and Windows Server 2003. If necessary, there are other applications such as XAMPP that are compatible with those systems.

Download and Install WAMP

STEP 1.   Download WAMPServer from http://www.wampserver.com/en/. If you are unsure whether your version of Windows is 32 or 64 Bit, choose 32 bit - it will run on either one.

STEP 2. Run the Installation. By default, the installer will choose Internet Explorer, you can change it later.

Launch WAMP Server

STEP 3. Click **WAMPServer** icon on the taskbar.
STEP 4. Click **phpmyadmin.**

Result: phpMyAdmin opens in a new window.

STEP 5. Click **Databases** in phpMyAdmin to create a new database.

Result: A new database information request appears.

STEP 6. Name the Database.
STEP 7. Click the **Create** button.

Results: The **www** directory will be automatically created (usually c:\wamp\www).

WordPress Files

STEP 8. Go to C:\wamp\www
STEP 9. Paste the WordPress folder there.
STEP 10. Rename the WordPress folder to your website name.

Results: The folder is renamed.

Configure WordPress

STEP 11. Go to the Web browser and go to http://localhost/sitename/ WordPress will display a message that it cannot find the wp_config.php file.

STEP 12. Click the **Create a Configuration File** button to create one.

STEP 13. On the Next Screen provide the database information;

       a.   The default database Username will be **Root**.

       b.   Leave the Password **Blank**.

STEP 14. Click **Submit** and WordPress will create a configuration file for you.

STEP 15. Click the **Run the Install** button.

Run the WordPress Installation

STEP 16. Fill out the installation form.

STEP 17. Provide the Title for the Website.

STEP 18. Provide the **Admin Username**, **Password**, and **Email Address**.

STEP 19. Click the **Install WordPress** button. A **Success** message will appear once WordPress creates the database tables.

STEP 20. Click the **Log In** button.

Permalinks for a Local Install

STEP 1.   Turn off the rewrite module in your WAMP installation.

STEP 2.   Go to **WAMP** icon in the taskbar.

STEP 3.   Go to **Apache → Apache Modules**.

STEP 4.   Go to **rewrite_module** and Click it to check it.

</THE END>

INDEX

www.ingramcontent.com/pod-product-compliance
Lightning Source LLC
Chambersburg PA
CBHW041005050326
40689CB00029B/4987